Praise for Arthur C. Brooks's *The Battle*

"[An] outstanding volume."
　　　　　—Ed Feulner, president, Heritage Foundation

"Clear, sharp, well reasoned and tough."
　　　　　—Karl Rove

"Brooks's key insight in *The Battle* is that the case for free enterprise is not materialism, but human flourishing."
　　　　　—Newt Gingrich

"Arthur Brooks is one of America's most astute, bold, and iconoclastic thinkers. *The Battle* provides yet more evidence of that fact."
　　　　　—William J. Bennett

"This is the playbook for the resurgence of the free enterprise movement."
　　　　　—former Vice President Dick Cheney

"Sometimes it takes someone who was on the other side to explain things clearly, as Brooks does in his eye-opening book."
　　　　　—Ron Kessler, Newsmax

"The book is a perfect Father's Day present and a great gift for any college grad or newly minted JD, MBA or MD who needs to understand the country's situation today."
　　　　　—radio show host Hugh Hewitt

"Brooks describes the players, outlines the stakes, and marshals the evidence that free enterprise produces richer, happier polities."
　　　　　—Matthew Continetti, *National Review*

"*The Battle* makes the moral case for enterprise . . . that the non-welfare state not only produces more wealth, but makes people happier, as happiness comes not from equality, but from self-fulfillment, as in 'earned success.'"
—*Washington Examiner*

"A fierce and necessary manifesto for the renewal of a common-sense right."
—Brian C. Anderson, *The American Spectator*

"*The Battle* is both a manifesto on behalf of the free enterprise system and a call to action for Americans to rally against the threats to it now emanating from Washington."
—James Pierson, *Claremont Review of Books*

"A timely reminder of the power of freedom."
—*St. Petersburg Times*

★ ★ ★ ★ ★

The
BATTLE

★ ★ ★ ★ ★

The
BATTLE

How the Fight Between
FREE ENTERPRISE and
BIG GOVERNMENT Will
Shape America's Future

ARTHUR C. BROOKS

BASIC BOOKS

A MEMBER OF THE PERSEUS BOOKS GROUP

New York

Designed by Jill Shaffer

The Library of Congress has cataloged the hardcover as follows:
Brooks, Arthur C., 1964-
    The battle : how the fight between free enterprise and big government
will shape America's future / Arthur C. Brooks.
        p.   cm.
    Includes bibliographical references and index.
    ISBN 978-0-465-01938-0
    1. Business and politics—United States. 2. Free enterprise—United
States. 3. Entrepreneurship—United States. I. Title.
    JK467.B76 2010
    322'.30973—dc22

                                                        2010008475

Paperback ISBN: 978-0-465-02212-0
e-book ISBN: 978-0-465-02787-3

10 9 8 7 6 5 4 3 2 1

*For my AEI colleagues, whose work
is a gift to America and the world*

Contents

Acknowledgments

M any people made this book a reality. The most important is my writing partner, Robin Currie, AEI's senior writer and editor, who collaborated with me on every part of this project. The book simply would not have been written without Robin, and if readers find elegant prose here, it is his. Amy Roden, AEI's program manager for economic policy studies, gave us first-rate data and research support, for which Robin and I are both deeply grateful. Tim Abbott was a summer intern at AEI in 2009 and also provided valuable help on the project. And my executive assistant, Kayla Cook, made this book possible while keeping day-to-day AEI work running smoothly.

I am truly indebted to my wonderful editor Lara Heimert at Basic Books and my literary agent, Lisa Adams, at the Garamond Agency. The rest of the Basic Books team, including John Sherer, Michele Jacob, Jessica Krakoski, and Ross Curley, made the whole project smooth and enjoyable.

Many of the ideas here were developed in articles published on the editorial page of the *Wall Street Journal*, for which I am thankful to Paul Gigot, Howard Dickman, and Rob Pollock.

For enriching my thinking in ways that are, I hope, reflected in this second edition of *The Battle*, my thanks go out to three extraordinary American thought-leaders. The first is *New York Times* columnist David Brooks, a great mind who challenged several of my assumptions in important ways. The second is Pete Wehner, my coauthor for *Wealth & Justice*, which (published between editions of *The Battle*) is effectively a companion volume to this book. The third is Representative Paul Ryan, with whom I have collaborated since the book was published and whose public service works out the practical implications of the free enterprise agenda every day.

Key insight for this project was provided by a number of my AEI colleagues: Jason Bertsch, Henry Olsen, Kevin Hassett, Danielle Pletka, David Gerson, and Chris DeMuth. Newt Gingrich encouraged and helped me through to the finish. AEI's redoubtable scholars provided the key arguments in the book; they were generous in their advice. These include Peter Wallison, Alex Pollock, Andrew Biggs, Charles Murray, Desmond Lachman, Alan Viard, Philip Levy, Adam Lerrick, and Karlyn Bowman. My colleagues Veronique Rodman, Nick Schulz, Toby Stock, Rachel Manfredi, Ellett George, and Carmela Aquino ensured the book and its message got into the right hands, as did Stephen Manfredi. I am grateful, too, for the input, trust, and support of AEI's outstanding board of trustees and its steadfast and generous donors.

Beyond AEI, I would like to express gratitude to a number of key individuals who helped with this book. In particular, I would like to thank Frank Hanna, Christopher Chandler, Ed Gillespie, Jim Clifton, Frank Newport, Carl Schramm, Bryan Caplan, R. G. Cook, Fr. Arne Panula, and Amity Shlaes.

Thanks also go out to those friends and supporters of AEI's vital work on the culture of free enterprise in America—among them, the Kern Family Foundation, Legatum, the Douglas and Maria DeVos Foundation, and the John Templeton Foundation. And also to the Kauffman Foundation, without whose vision and support, research on entrepreneurship would not be where it is today.

Finally, no acknowledgments are complete without thanking my wife and fellow free enterprise enthusiast, Ester. As an immigrant, Ester has taught me why American freedom is so valuable and profound. If this book creates value, the reward to Ester and me will be in knowing that the free-enterprise system is a little safer and stronger for our three children, Joaquim, Carlos, and Marina.

Foreword

THE CHOICE, THE FACTS, AND THE ARGUMENT:

Why *The Battle: How the Fight Between Free Enterprise and Big Government Will Shape America's Future* Is One of the Most Important Books in Your Lifetime

BY NEWT GINGRICH

A RTHUR C. BROOKS has written a book that will take its place with Charles Murray's *Losing Ground* as one of the pivotal books around which American history turned.

From his very first sentences Brooks outlines a stark and compelling analysis of the crisis of contemporary America.

Brooks begins, "America faces a new culture war. This is not the culture war of the 1990s. This is not a fight over guns, abortions, religion, and gays. Nor is it about Republicans versus Democrats. Rather, it is a struggle between two competing visions of America's future."

The Battle then addresses three big facts:

First, there is a fundamental disagreement about America's future between a socialist, redistributionist minority (the 30 percent coalition) and a massive free enterprise, work ethic, opportunity-oriented majority (the 70 percent majority). For years I have spoken and written that "we are the majority." It is a concept I learned from Ronald Reagan in the 1970s. Now Brooks provides the ammunition to factually explain why the 70 percent should govern America as a reflection of our legitimate majority status.

Second, there is an elite system of power that enables the 30 percent coalition to dominate the 70 percent majority. There are the seeds of an extraordinary history book buried in a few paragraphs of *The Battle*. How did the coalition of word users come to so thoroughly dominate the coalition of workers and doers? How did the elites on academic campuses come to define legitimacy for the news media, the Hollywood system, the courts, and the bureaucracy? Brooks makes clear that the dominance of the hard left in these worlds is a fact. He sets the stage for someone (maybe another AEI scholar) to develop the historic explanation of how this usurpation of the people by the elite came to be.

Third, this is a conflict over values in which those who represent redistributionist, left-wing materialism have stolen the language of morality while those who favor freedom, individual opportunity, the right to pursue happiness, and personal liberty have been maneuvered into a series of banal and ultimately unattractive positions in the public debate. Brooks's outline of a morally dominant culture of freedom shaming the materialistic, statist, coercive culture of redistribution is as important for our generation as Hayek's *The Road to Serfdom* was for the Reagan-Thatcher generation.

What makes *The Battle* so important is its unique combination of intellectual clarity and the best succinct analysis of the values of the American people I have ever read.

Brooks argues that conservatism—in its market-oriented, individual liberty, equality of opportunity, right to pursue happiness, and work ethic form—is both popular and historically the most positive way for people to live.

After you have read this book and committed its arguments and its salient facts to memory, you will be able to debate any elitist redistributionist leftist and win the day in both moral rhetoric and factual analysis.

Every American concerned about their country's future and worried by the radicalism of the Obama-Pelosi-Reid machine should read *The Battle*. It is the ammunition with which to save our country and change our history for the better.

Introduction

THIS IS A BOOK about American culture. I don't mean traditional "culture issues," such as religion, abortion, and homosexual rights. Rather, it is a book about the true center of what makes our culture exceptional and different from others: free enterprise.

Free enterprise is the system characterized by individual liberty over collectivism, earned success over entitlement, and private entrepreneurship over government control. This book will make the case that free enterprise is truly mainstream, is loved by Americans for nonmaterialist reasons, and is a fundamental key to our happiness as a people. However, I do not expect you to accept or reject my arguments based on any subjective criteria. In this book, I will prove these arguments—to my satisfaction and, I hope, to yours too—not with theory or philosophy or ideology but with *data* on public opinion, economic prosperity, and (most important) human happiness.

I originally published this book in the summer of 2010, after the Obama administration had established itself but before the 2010 midterm election. It was a time of dramatic turmoil: This period saw the rise of the grassroots Tea Party movement against big government in America. The movement, which Gallup polls show was supported by fully one-third of Americans and was seen favorably by a large majority, was not a demand for government jobs or services during a terrible recession. It was a rebellion *against* the expansion of government.[1]

The Tea Party protests were nothing less than a manifestation of true American cultural exceptionalism. In 2009 and 2010, protesters in Greece, France, Spain, and Portugal were taking to the streets, demanding an end to fiscal austerity and a continuation of absurdly early retirement ages and lavish state pensions. In short, they were insisting income and benefits be redistributed from their fellow citizens amid the worst recession in decades. In America, in contrast, protesters were demanding an *end* to fiscal profligacy and government expansion.

The first edition of this book suggested that a major political wave was in the works, with the culture of free enterprise at its core. And the following November, 242 Republicans took back the House of Representatives. It was the biggest midterm gain in House seats for either party since 1938. The Republicans only narrowly missed taking back the Senate from the Democrats, increased their share of governorships from 23 to 29, and gained a record 680 seats in state legislatures. And these were not the apparatchik Republicans of old. The Republican Study Committee, which contains the House of Representatives' fiscal conservative caucus, swelled from 115 members before the election to 176 afterward. The GOP House leader John Boehner called the election "a repudiation of Washington," and President Obama agreed, calling it "a shellacking."

It's still too early to tell whether the November 2010 election will change the political orientation of the current administration. Some early indications are that President Obama is moving his policies and staff more to the center as a result. If the midterm results lead to the president refocusing more on free enterprise in the second half of his term, it will be good for America and good for his reelection chances in 2012.

In the wake of the 2010 election, three explanations emerged for what had happened—two incorrect and one correct. The first came from many triumphalist Republicans, who saw in the victory a resuscitation of the Republican brand. But understandable as it was, this was a dangerous misinterpretation. Indeed, on the brink of the midterms, polls showed that 42 percent of Americans had a negative attitude toward the Democratic Party—and *43 percent* a negative attitude toward the Republican Party.

Fortunately for Republicans, this explanation was not shared by the new House leaders, who were contrite about past failures and determined not to display hubris at the victory. "I don't necessarily see it as an election in favor of Republicans," noted Wisconsin Republican congressman Paul Ryan. "I see it as an election opposed to the direction in which the president and his party have taken the country, which was in a very big government direction."

Unfortunately for Democrats, their party's leadership was less humble. Instead, they reelected their House leader, liberal

San Francisco congresswoman Nancy Pelosi, and embraced a second mistaken interpretation of the election results. As many Democrats explained it to me and others, no real shift had taken place, and there was no mandate for change. All that had happened was a little conservative brainwashing of the unreliable political middle. Under this view, there are 50 or 60 seats in the House of Representatives that tend to fluctuate between the Democratic Party and the GOP. The Democrats gained 31 of these seats in 2006 and picked up another 21 in 2008. In 2010, the awful labor market in the United States led Americans (who were too impatient and ill-informed to understand the Democrats' beneficial economic policies) simply to flip these seats plus a few more back to the Republicans.

This explanation attributes no blame whatsoever to ideology and makes no acknowledgment of any popular rebellion against what the elites were doing in this country. It also allows its adherents to keep making the principled case for what they are doing, to stick with the same agenda, and to maintain the same leadership. In short, it enables them to continue to occupy what they consider the moral high ground in America and to continue to move us in the direction of European-style social democracy.

The third explanation for the midterm election is the one prefigured in this book, in its explanation of the 2008 election. In a nutshell, Americans in 2008 had punished an unprincipled Republican party—a party that had failed to prevent an economic crisis, then reacted to it with bailouts of car companies and deficit-driven, state-expanding stimulus spending. But the political left that came to office after the 2008 election delivered exactly the opposite of what most Americans wanted. The deficit expanded, the state grew, and regulation exploded. Entrepreneurs found it harder to operate, and businesspeople felt vilified if they earned a profit during tough times. Ordinary Americans saw makers penalized and takers rewarded, with bailouts for poorly managed companies and homeowners who had made irresponsible borrowing decisions. The government-sponsored enterprises (GSEs)—"Fannie" and "Freddie"—that had sparked the housing crisis were empowered instead of dismantled.

A new kind of ethical populism swept America. In a now-famous televised rant on the floor of the Chicago Board of Trade in February 2009, CNBC correspondent Rick Santelli shouted, "The government is promoting bad behavior." As those around him applauded, he continued, "This is America! How many of you people want to pay for your neighbors' mortgage that has an extra bathroom and can't pay their bills? . . . President Obama, are you listening?"

Whether he was listening or not, the president's handling of the economy plummeted in popularity, and the Democratic Congress's favorability fell even further, at its lowest point in December 2010 scraping 13 percent, a level usually reserved for enemy nations and the Internal Revenue Service.[2]

Curiously to some, the most overt protesters were not the poor and unemployed. Nor were they rich people trying to avoid the punitive tax increases advocated by the governing political left. They were employed, middle-class folks, unlikely to face either joblessness or higher taxes, but still outraged by what they saw as increasingly statist policies from Washington. Liberal pundits and politicians opined that this was a result of some sort of "false consciousness" on the part of the protesters or a conspiracy to fool the public by conservative news outlets. "This is not grass roots," pronounced then–Senate majority leader Harry Reid, holding up a square of bright green Astroturf. The demonstrations were, he said, "about as phony as this grass."[3]

But in truth, there was no conspiracy at work. The real story is the one in this book: Free enterprise is fundamental to whom we believe we are as a people. Our system is not primarily about money but about freedom and flourishing. The questions we face are *cultural*, not financial. And politicians, Republicans or Democrats, meddle with our culture of free enterprise at their peril.

The cultural disagreements discussed in this book were (and are) so strong, in fact, that I consider the 2010 midterm election a skirmish in the new "culture war" in America. The conflict implied in this metaphor is not (and I believe never will be) a violent one, but rather a vigorous competition of ideas that is fundamental to a free society. Indeed, the fact that a book like this can be published is evidence of the fact that the American system—despite our disagreements—is still healthy.

The Battle does not advocate this new culture war—it merely identifies it. The redistributive policies of the recent past and the open statism of our political leaders have provoked it. And now, that conflict is playing out all around us. It determined the outcome of the 2010 election and is defining the issues at stake in the momentous policy debates of 2011 and 2012.

This book highlights the consequences of acquiescing to statism and effectively abandoning our free-enterprise culture. It also shows how dangerously far down that road we have traveled. Since the book was published, the situation has arguably gotten worse, not better, and the advancement of a few free-enterprise politicians gives little reason to revise that estimation. The federal debt continues to skyrocket and is now at its highest level since the end of World War II. As I write these words, our federal government owes $13.9 trillion, which is the equivalent of $45,000 for every citizen in the country. This year alone, the U.S. government will spend at least $1.3 trillion more than it raises, and that doesn't include the hundreds of billions overspent by state and local governments. The communist Chinese own nearly $900 billion of our national debt. In America, 9.7 percent of total gross domestic product (GDP) goes to entitlements, which are still off limits to any discretionary spending cuts. Social Security is the biggest of these federal spending programs and the largest tax paid by most American workers, whereas Medicare costs us around $450 billion per year—that's more than $1,450 for every man, woman, and child in the United States.

Current levels of entitlement spending are unsustainable—and if we do nothing, the crisis is only going to get worse. With an aging population and rising health-care costs, entitlements will continue to spiral upward, reaching about 14.4 percent of

GDP by 2030. If Americans do nothing, politicians will interpret this as tacit acceptance of their statist agenda.

Worse yet, America's culture will change. At some tipping point, the net takers will simply overwhelm the makers in a country that has a shrinking tax base but expensive government largesse, spread around without regard for need. For the moment, we are a nation ethically committed to freedom, merit, and entrepreneurship. But only vigilance will guarantee that this remains the case. Already, one public opinion indicator has emerged since the original publication of this book that shows a "softening" in our free-enterprise culture. In January 2011, the Republican-leaning organization Resurgent Republic asked a large sample of Americans which of the following statements comes closer to their view: (a) government should do more to solve problems and help meet the needs of people; or (b) government is trying to do more things than it can do well, things that should be left to the private sector and individuals. Forty-nine percent of respondents chose (a); 46 percent chose (b).[4]

For the most part, we are still a country strongly committed to free enterprise. But whether or not this continues to be the case is in our own hands. A year after the publication of this book, the battle for free enterprise goes on. One midterm election does not change this fact—and provides no room for complacency. On the contrary, now is when the real work of reform begins, when we point America back in the direction of its free-enterprise roots.

CHAPTER ONE

The 70–30 Nation

A MERICA faces a new culture war.

This is not the culture war of the 1990s. This is not a fight over guns, abortions, religion, and gays. Nor is it about Republicans versus Democrats. Rather, it is a struggle between two competing visions of America's future. In one, America will continue to be a unique and exceptional nation organized around the principles of free enterprise. In the other, America will move toward European-style statism grounded in expanding bureaucracies, increasing income redistribution, and government-controlled corporations. These competing visions are not reconcilable: We must choose.

The battle between free enterprise and statism is not a minor one to be debated by economists. This is not an argument over financial details or government accounting minutiae. It is not a small difference of opinion over a couple of percentage points in marginal tax rates. This is about whether America will move toward social democracy like many other developed nations or will remain the America of entrepreneurs, individual opportunity, and limited government.

The proponents of statism are not evil or stupid, but I believe they are wrong about what is best for our nation. This book will present the evidence that free enterprise is an expression of the core values of a large majority of Americans. It brings the most life satisfaction to the most people. Personal liberty, individual opportunity, and entrepreneurship are the explanation for our nation's past success and the promise of greater things to come.

But the unprecedented economic crisis introduced panic to our nation. Panic distorted our values and gave the minority who oppose free enterprise a pretext to introduce sweeping change. Many of our current leaders, and the vocal and influential group who supports them, eschew the value of free enterprise and seek to make our country more statist and redistributive.

It is not at all clear which side will prevail in the struggle over free enterprise. Large numbers of Americans have forgotten the evils of Soviet socialism and the disasters of the Great Society's welfare state programs in this country. The forces of statism swept into office in 2008 with a vengeance, and many still hold office today. They have had the full arsenal of government money and power, they are working for the hearts of a whole generation of younger Americans, and they have used our economic insecurity to introduce breathtaking increases in state power. They are playing for keeps, and if they win, America will change forever.

This is a book about free enterprise, so let's start by defining it. *Free enterprise* is the system of values and laws that respects private property, encourages industry, celebrates liberty, limits government, and creates individual opportunity. Under free enterprise, people can pursue their own ends—and they reap the rewards and consequences, positive and negative, of their own actions.[1]

Free enterprise has been integral to American culture from our nation's earliest days. As we all know, liberty was a constant aspiration of the founders—freedom from coercion, or as they put it, from "tyranny." Again and again the founders return to liberty: "They who can give up essential liberty to obtain a little temporary safety, deserve neither liberty nor safety," declared Benjamin Franklin. And Patrick Henry warned: "Guard with jealous attention the public liberty. Suspect every one who approaches that jewel."

Free enterprise gave the founders' beloved liberty natural expression in the everyday life and work of American citizens. Despite the difficulties of agricultural life in early America and the hardships of the industrial revolution, Americans came to enjoy—through free markets for goods, services, and their own labor—small expressions of liberty in all the ordinary, prosaic details of their economic lives.

Through free enterprise, Americans were able truly to live their liberty. *They*, not their government, were in charge of their economic lives when they chose their own professions or started their own businesses—unthinkable things for so many ordinary people in Europe at the time. "A wise and frugal Government, which shall restrain men from injuring one another," Thomas Jefferson famously declared in his first inaugural address in 1801, "shall leave them otherwise free to regulate their own pursuits of industry and improvement." But even in America, he later warned, beware the state's attempts to short-circuit the rewards of economic liberty: "To take from one, because it is thought his own industry and that of his fathers has acquired too much, in order to spare to others, who, or whose fathers, have not exercised equal industry and skill, is to violate arbitrarily the first principle of association, the guarantee to everyone the free exercise of his industry and the fruits acquired by it."[2]

Jefferson said this, and Americans actually lived it. It did not take long for outsiders to realize how exceptional America's culture of free enterprise was. The French nobleman Alexis de Tocqueville called Americans "the freest people in the world." During his nine-month stay in America, he was struck by two characteristics of these "exceptional people." The first was their determination to single-mindedly pursue their own interests and enterprises under the supervision of a limited government. The second was their willingness to band together voluntarily for community and civic action.[3]

Tocqueville was particularly struck by the enormous contrast between the free-enterprise culture of America and what he saw in Europe: "Wherever at the head of some new undertaking you see the government in France, or a man of rank in England," he wrote in *Democracy in America* (1835), "in the United States you will be sure to find an association."[4]

Tocqueville's distinction between Americans and Europeans remains accurate to this day. When it comes to attitudes about free enterprise, there are stark differences between Americans and our cousins across the Atlantic. According to a 2006 Pew Research Center Global Attitudes Survey, Europeans are half as likely as Americans to attribute success in life to their own efforts. They are far less likely to say that competition is a positive force for the country. And they value less the merits of personal industry: Even the notoriously industrious Germans are only one-third as likely as Americans (20 percent compared to 60 percent) to believe that children should be instructed in the value of hard work.[5]

Entrepreneurship was and is the purest expression of America's free-enterprise culture and the essence of the American Dream. Nothing is more prototypical of American culture than an admiration for earned success through entrepreneurship. Indeed, the nineteenth-century author Horatio Alger became an iconic cultural figure not for any sort of literary excellence, but because the protagonists of his novels were shoe-shiners, newsboys, and street musicians who—through hard work and clever ideas—rose from rags to riches.[6]

Entrepreneurship is so central to American culture that some have even suggested that Americans are genetically predisposed to it. And this might well be true. A great deal of recent work by psychologists on twins and other siblings has demonstrated that our personalities are significantly determined by our genes—for instance, up to 80 percent of our happiness is innate. Likewise, nearly half of our religiosity and half our political ideology can be explained by nature instead of nurture.[7]

So entrepreneurship, as a personality trait, might be in the American DNA. Think about it: Immigrants tend to be entrepreneurial, willing to give up security and familiarity for the possibility of prosperity and success. This trait is relatively rare—a mutation from the norm. Only a small minority of people from any particular community tend to migrate away from their homeland. But the United States is a nation made up of such people, a land where immigrants and their descendants have married other immigrants and their descendants. Consequently, a genetic mutation that leads to entrepreneurial behavior would appear in more of our citizens and replicate itself much more easily than elsewhere. As a result, America's vast success might be explained in part by our genetic predisposition to embrace risks with potentially explosive rewards.

Even if entrepreneurship can be partially explained by genetics, the founders would no doubt remind us that it can't be taken for granted. It can flourish only where there is a good economic culture—one in which there is a high level of willingness on the part of individuals to innovate and exert leadership. People within such a culture also have to possess a high tolerance level for uncertainty and risk in their lives—a willingness to gamble the securities and shortcomings of the status quo for the chance of future success or possible failure.

A good economic culture also requires a wise and limited government, as Jefferson always emphasized. We need efficient and fairly applied legal and regulatory systems and well-defined property rights. We have to let people succeed and let people fail.[8]

Free enterprise lies at the very core of America's national history, culture, and character. Most of us believe that free enterprise is the best system for America. It is part of the cultural mainstream—as American as apple pie.

Most people have a story of their own personal change and growth that they attribute to the freedoms our free-enterprise system has bestowed. In my own case, the flexibility of free markets and a merit-based culture allowed me to drop out of college, make my living as a musician for 12 years, drop back into school to study economics, work for a decade as a university professor—and then run a Washington think tank. Unthinkable in most countries, my own story is not really that exceptional in America.

No matter what the data source or how we formulate the questions, we see that Americans love free enterprise. Whether we ask people their views about free markets, the importance of private business, or the proper role of government and taxation, a very large majority express support for free enterprise over statism and redistribution.

The Free-Enterprise System

Americans prefer capitalism over socialism. A January 2010 Gallup poll surveyed respondents about their views on the two systems. It found that 61 percent of Americans hold a positive view of capitalism, while about the same percentage have a negative view of socialism. The older the age group, the more negative the view of socialism.[9]

Of course, *capitalism* and *socialism* are charged terms. The choice of words may influence the results of a survey. The results are even stronger using the term *free markets*. In March 2009, the nonpartisan Pew Research Center asked individuals from a broad range of American demographic groups the following question: "Generally, do you think people are better off in a free market economy, even though there may be severe ups and downs from time to time, or don't you think so?" The results are decisive: Almost 70 percent of respondents agree that they are better off in a free market economy. Only 20 percent disagree with the statement that America is better off with a free market economy.[10]

Free enterprise is even more popular than capitalism and free markets. In the same Gallup poll mentioned above, a stunning 86 percent have a positive image of free enterprise. Only 10 percent have a negative image. Similarly, 84 percent have a positive image of entrepreneurs, while just 10 percent see them negatively.

In sum, no matter how the question is posed, less than 30 percent of Americans say they believe we would be better off without free enterprise at the core of our system.

Taxation

It is no surprise that in a country devoted to the free-enterprise system, people believe the government takes too much money away from us. Although polls find a visceral sympathy for increasing taxes on "the rich," the data show that most Americans believe the maximum fair tax level is far below what the upper classes are currently paying.

By a large margin, Americans feel overtaxed. According to an April 2009 poll by the Tax Foundation, 56 percent of U.S. adults believe their federal income taxes are "too high." Only one-third believe that the amount of taxes they pay is "about right." Just 2 percent—people I have never met—say their taxes are too low.[11]

Yes, some surveys suggest that in America there is popular support for increasing taxes on the rich. Two-thirds of those polled in a FOX News/Opinion Dynamics survey in March 2009 favored raising taxes on households earning more than $250,000 a year if taxes were lowered for other households.[12]

But these statistics are misleading: If you dig deeper into the data, the popularity of "tax the rich" politics begins to crumble. Another spring 2009 poll found that 69 percent of Americans think the top federal tax rate should be 20 percent or lower. Even 62 percent of Democrats think this. But of course, the top federal income tax rate is not less than 20 percent. It is currently 35 percent and will rise under the Democrats' tax plan—and will be made worse by the fact that their plan phases out tax deductions.[13]

Americans do not realize that we are a high-tax country already. When they learn how much we are currently taking from our citizens—even "the rich"—they think it is too much.

Business

Attitudes toward commerce are another barometer of American attitudes toward free enterprise. Much has been made in the media of the immense unpopularity of "big business" in America, with some polls showing up to 68 percent disapproval.[14]

Americans are understandably wary of American big business practices. This is especially true in the wake of revelations about the corporate governance—particularly in the elite financial sector—that has done immense damage to the U.S. economy. A 2009 Pew Values Survey found that 77 percent of Americans say too much power is concentrated in the hands of a few big companies, and two-thirds believe that "Wall Street only cares about making money for itself."[15]

Still, these numbers don't tell the true story. The same Pew study found that 76 percent of Americans believe that the strength of this country is mostly based on the success of American business—a percentage that has remained consistent for over a decade. In 2010, Gallup found that 66 percent of Americans believe that when big business earns a profit, it helps the economy, while just 18 percent think it hurts the economy.[16]

Clearly, most Americans support the private sector and its ability to generate wealth. But they are not entirely trusting of big business. America's overwhelming support for free enterprise is not equivalent to blind support for corporations—which makes perfect sense. As my wife told me when I showed her the preceding data on Americans' mixed attitudes about business, "It's just like marriage: Everybody thinks it's a great institution, but nobody trusts husbands." Similarly, a healthy love of capitalism does not require a naïve belief that all capitalists are good and honest.

However, any mistrust there is of American big business has led to little support for the institutions that attack it most vigorously: labor unions and government regulators. A 2009 Labor Day Gallup poll found that 51 percent of Americans believe unions hurt rather than help the nation's economy. Gallup also asked Americans in February 2010 if they are more worried by too much regulation of business by government or by not enough regulation. Their response? Fifty-seven percent are worried by too much regulation, 37 percent by not enough.[17]

And despite some misgivings about big business, Americans *love* small business. The 2010 Gallup survey found that 95 percent of Americans have a positive image of small business. One doubts whether motherhood would even score so well.

Government

The image of business in America may be tarnished today, but the majority of Americans still vastly prefer it to government. Even as the unemployment rate in the private sector soared in January 2010, Gallup found that six in ten Americans said they would rather work for business than for government.[18]

Most Americans believe the government actually hinders more than it assists us. In January 2009, the Pew Economic Mobility Project asked approximately 2,000 Americans, "Do you think the government does more to help or more to hurt people trying to move up the economic ladder?" Even amid the most frightening economic crisis in decades, more people said the government would hurt than people who thought it would help (50 percent versus 39 percent).[19]

Americans are least supportive of government when it redistributes income and penalizes the successful. An April 2009 survey by the polling firm Ayers-McHenry asked registered voters which of the following statements about the role of government came closer to their view:

(a) Government policies should promote fairness by narrowing the gap between rich and poor, spreading the wealth, and making sure that economic outcomes are more equal.

(b) Government policies should promote opportunity by fostering job growth, encouraging entrepreneurs, and allowing people to keep more of what they earn. Whereas 31 percent opted for (a), 63 percent chose (b).[20]

Although the data are mixed about how much we think the government should provide us in services (and there is evidence that our taste for government services may be rising), Americans generally prefer less government when they are confronted with the need to pay for it. When the Ayers-McHenry poll asked, "Overall, would you prefer larger government with more services and higher taxes, or smaller government with fewer services and lower taxes?" 21 percent favored larger government, while 69 percent preferred smaller government. Similarly, the 2006 General Social Survey asked,

"Do you believe there should be cuts in government spending?" Sixty-three percent of Americans are in favor of this idea, while only 14 percent are against it.[21]

Americans don't want more government activity because they have little trust in the public sector. A CBS/*New York Times* poll in February 2010 found that 81 percent of Americans believe they cannot trust the federal government or that they can trust it only some of the time. Just 16 percent say they can trust it most of the time. A similar CNN/Opinion Research Corporation poll in December 2008 found corresponding results of 66 and 22 percent.[22]

Whether we look at capitalism, taxes, business, or government, the data show a clear and consistent pattern: 70 percent of Americans support the free-enterprise system and are unsupportive of big government. By contrast, somewhere between 20 and 30 percent of the adult population opposes free enterprise and prefers government solutions to our problems. To be generous, let's round up to 30 percent, and call them the "30 percent coalition."

Who is in the 30 percent coalition? There are two groups: leaders and followers.

The 30 percent coalition is led by people who are smart, powerful, and strategic. These are many of the people who make opinions, entertain us, inform us, and teach our kids in college. They are the intellectual upper class: those in the top 5 percent of the population in income; who hold graduate degrees; and who work in intellectual industries, such as law, education, journalism, and entertainment.

The intellectual upper class is far more statist and left-wing than the average American, and is getting more so. Consider the evidence: Across most of the socioeconomic spectrum, Americans have trended more conservative over the past three decades. The nonintellectual upper class (engineers, bankers, and the like), the middle class, the working class, and the lower class have all trended right since the 1970s. But the intellectual upper class has bucked the conservative trend: The National Opinion Research Center's General Social Survey shows, among high-income, high-education individuals in intellectual professions, that the percentage of self-described "liberals" minus "conservatives" increased approximately twentyfold since 1972.[23]

The intellectual upper class has become the most important party in the 30 percent coalition—the chief adversary of the free-enterprise system today. And at the head of the intellectual upper class are many of our current leaders in Washington, DC.

Here's an insight on our own president's thoughts on the free-enterprise system, spoken in his own words to the graduating seniors of Arizona State University at their commencement ceremony on May 13, 2009: "You're taught to chase after the usual brass rings, being on this 'who's who' list or that top 100 list; how much money you make and how big your corner office is; whether you have a fancy enough title or a nice enough car. . . . Let me suggest that such an approach won't get you where you want to go. It displays a poverty of ambition."[24]

Conservatives and liberals argued for months about President Obama's intent in this speech. Many people found it to be a repudiation of American free-enterprise culture. Our drive to achieve is part and parcel of the American Dream—the belief that we can be successful, however we measure that success—and that our kids can be even *more* successful. For many Americans, if that means producing a lot (and then earning a lot), that's our business and nobody else's. The fact that we so doggedly seek success in our enterprises—denominated in money or however we like—is what Tocqueville thought made American culture exceptional.

Other cultural leaders in the intellectual upper class at the vanguard of the 30 percent coalition include those from academia, the media, and the entertainment industry. All the data available tell us that these industries are among the most radical in the battle against our culture of free enterprise.

Academia is a particularly important part of the 30 percent coalition. Academics as a whole align massively with the far left—more so than any other profession, according to General Social Survey data from 1996 to 2008. A 2002 study examined the political ideology of social science professors in a number of our nation's top universities. At Cornell, for example, 166 were liberal and 6 conservative. At the University of Colorado, 116 were liberal and 5 conservative.[25]

Academic hostility to capitalism is legendary. Even in academic fields typically considered congenial to free enterprise, we find significant opposition to the values of 70 percent of Americans. One recent study examined the policy views of members of the American Economic Association, the professional body to which economics professors belong. The study's findings are stark: Only 8 percent of economists can be considered supporters of free market principles; less than 3 percent of them, strong supporters.[26]

Journalists are a tremendously influential component of the 30 percent coalition as well. When asked in a 2005 poll about their political views, nearly three times as many journalists described themselves as liberals as those who described themselves as conservatives.[27]

As lopsided as it is, however, the news media is no match for the entertainment industry when it comes to hostility toward traditional free-enterprise culture. "Capitalism is an evil, and you cannot regulate evil. You have to eliminate it and replace it with something that is good for all people and that something is democracy." So says Michael Moore, the infamous filmmaker at the end of his latest documentary, *Capitalism: A Love Story*.[28]

Moore's is not an aberrant view in Hollywood. The General Social Survey mentioned above that ranked academia as the most liberal of occupations listed "creative artists" at number three (with "authors and journalists" at number two). In the 2008 election cycle, 78 percent of entertainment industry political donations went to Democrats and 22 percent to Republicans. For good reason, former White House chief of staff Rahm Emanuel once declared, "You can't run for president as a Democrat and not have a foothold in Hollywood."[29]

If you count up all the statist politicians, socialist college professors, left-leaning journalists, America-bashing entertainers, and others in the intellectual elite, that still doesn't come to more than a few percent of the population. It's nowhere near

30 percent. To get to that number, we have to turn our attention away from the leaders and consider the followers. That means millions and millions of ordinary folks. Where do we look for them?

There are some predicable geographic enclaves, such as San Francisco, California, in which 64 percent of residents call themselves "liberal" or "very liberal" (compared with 29 percent of adults nationwide). Similar lopsided ideology comes from such liberal havens as Seattle, Washington, and Boulder, Colorado.[30]

But the real core of the 30 percent coalition is not San Franciscans but young people all over America—adults under 30. This is not just a fifth of the adult population: It is the future of our country. And this group has exhibited a frightening openness to statism and redistribution.

Socialism may sound bad to you, but it is not a dirty word to many of today's young people. In March 2009, the Pew Research Center asked people to choose between capitalism and socialism. For those over the age of 40, only 13 percent choose socialism. For adults under 30, however, the results are different: Younger Americans are almost evenly divided, with 37 percent favoring capitalism, 33 percent favoring socialism, and 30 percent not sure (and thus open to persuasion). A January 2010 Gallup poll found that a majority of young adults between the ages of 18 and 34 hold a positive view of socialism.[31]

Predictably, during the 2008 presidential campaign, Republican charges that Barack Obama had socialistic impulses had no perceptible electoral impact on young people. According to election exit polls, Barack Obama cleaned John McCain's clock among young voters—66 percent to 32 percent.[32]

Perhaps all of this is understandable. To anyone over 40, the word *socialism* brings immediately to mind the humanity-crushing evils of the Soviet empire. Socialism was the banner under which tens of millions were killed and hundreds of millions more were subjugated. But now consider a 25-year-old, born in 1985. The Soviet Union fell apart when she was six years old, and the only true socialists she has ever encountered were her college professors. For 45-year-olds like me, socialism means gulags. To 25-year-olds, it means boring but harmless middle-aged guys with beards and PhDs.

For whatever reason, young people don't find socialism inherently repellent. This is an enormous opening for the 30 percent coalition.

The political left understands the 30 percent coalition's appeal among young adults. It aggressively and successfully wooed them in the 2008 election campaigns and plans to grow its coalition over time.

There are three long-term strategies to keep the young in the 30 percent coalition: pay off their debts, give them government jobs, and make sure they never have to pay for the services that the government provides.

First, pay off their debts. In his 2010 State of the Union speech, President Obama offered to cancel student loan debts for those who put in ten years working for federal, state, or local governments or who worked for nonprofit organizations. The proposed plan will also forgive student loans for people in the private sector—but not for twenty years.

For the 30 percent coalition, therefore, bureaucrats deserve better treatment from the government than entrepreneurs. If you start your own business, you have to pay off your debts. But if *I* go to work for the IRS to tax *your* business, I get my debts forgiven—by my own employer. What better way to influence a whole generation?[33]

Second, pass out government jobs. In 2009, the federal government added 13,000 jobs to the rolls. And high-paying jobs at that: The number of federal salaries over $150,000 per year more than doubled since the recession began in 2007. Today, the average total compensation for federal workers is nearly $14,000 per year more than for equivalent private sector workers. To find this acceptable, you must agree that the average federal worker is much more productive or deserving than the average person in the private sector.[34]

Third, reduce their taxes so young people have no incentive to resist the expansion of statism. Federal tax policies are ensuring that an increasing number of people in our society will never develop a pocketbook interest in free enterprise. Even as they grow older, develop their careers, and earn more money, many will never pay a dollar in federal income tax because they'll never catch up with an increasingly progressive tax system.

To put a modern twist on an old axiom, a man who is not a socialist at 20 has no heart. But a man who is still a socialist at

40 has no head—or pays no taxes. The current trend will increase the percentage of Americans who are permanent net takers from our society, who use more in public resources than they contribute, and for whom a free-enterprise system of entrepreneurship and limited government holds few obvious personal rewards. In a nutshell, the strategy is to make fewer and fewer people pay all the taxes and bear the brunt of paying for a growing government.

The redistributionists have already been remarkably successful in this effort. In 1986, the top 10 percent of income earners paid 55 percent of the federal income taxes in the United States, and the bottom 90 percent paid 45 percent. By 2006, the top 10 percent were paying about 71 percent of the taxes, while the bottom 90 percent were paying 29 percent. And in case you're wondering, the top 10 percent's share of taxes is 50 percent larger than its share of the income. Meanwhile, the bottom 50 percent's income share is four times the size of its tax share.[35]

The percentage of Americans paying *nothing* in income taxes is also rising. Most people (66 percent) agree with the proposition that everybody should pay *something*, even if it's just a pro forma contribution to the government so they remember it isn't free. Yet despite this strongly held sentiment, an increasing number of Americans pay nothing.[36]

The federal government has plans to increase dramatically the percentage of nonpayers. In early 2009, before the economic stimulus package was enacted into law, 38 percent of

Americans were estimated to have zero or negative federal income tax liability. (Negative taxes are paid by people receiving refundable tax credits and similar subsidies from the government, such as the Earned Income Tax Credit.) After President Obama's budget stimulus and the proposed tax changes of 2011 (which were ultimately postponed, but not canceled), this proportion will increase to almost 47 percent. Economists estimate that another 11 percent will pay less than 5 percent of their income in federal income taxes and less than $1,000 in total.[37]

Simply stated, in the future there will be fewer and fewer people with "skin in the game." Nonpayers will outnumber the payers. We will eventually reach a threshold beyond which most Americans have no economic incentive to defend free enterprise because it is so far from their interest to do so. The young sympathizers of socialism today may be the grown-up defenders of socialism tomorrow.

These are three powerful strategies to increase the 30 percent coalition. Still, they all take a long time to come to fruition. It would require a couple of generations to truly transform America from a nation of makers into a nation of takers. Fortunately for the 30 percent coalition, however, a once-in-a-lifetime game-changer came along—one that they believed could flip millions over to the 30 percent's viewpoint about free enterprise in a matter of months, if they played their cards right.

Perhaps you're thinking that the game-changer was the 2008 election that gave the Democrats control over the executive branch and both houses of Congress. You would be mistaken. Statism had effectively taken hold in Washington long before that.

It was a Republican-led government that began the huge Wall Street and Detroit bailouts. This raised expectations about future levels of spending that the incoming administration was able to fulfill. And for years before the crisis, Republicans weakened the culture of free enterprise, just as Democrats did. During those years, the GOP talked about free enterprise while simultaneously growing the government with borrowed money and increasing the percentage of citizens with no income tax liability. These legislators spent billions of tax dollars on special interests with every bit as much gusto as any statist on the left.

Why would candidates who ran in favor of free enterprise govern in this way? Why abandon the principles of the 70 percent majority and start behaving like the other members of the 30 percent coalition once they are in power? The best explanation is right there: *power*. Politicians have their hands on your money—and they like to spend it.

"The natural progress of things," Thomas Jefferson warned, "is for liberty to yield and government to gain ground." Politicians and policymakers may arrive in Washington, DC, with a particular ideology and plans to reform government, but after a few terms, they usually "go native." Democrats and Republicans alike realize that their real role is to exercise power and that in Washington that means spending power.[38]

Look at social spending at the federal level—always a target of Republicans running for office. From 2001 to 2008, when the GOP occupied the White House and during part of which they also controlled the Senate and the House of Representatives, these expenditures rose. Even after adjusting for inflation, for example, the Department of Education grew by 54 percent.[39]

It doesn't stop there. Consider new entitlements such as Medicare Part D, the program to give prescription drugs to seniors, passed in a bipartisan process in 2003. The Medicare Modernization Act became the largest medical entitlement program in history. The Congressional Budget Office estimated that its cost to taxpayers from 2004 to 2013 would be $593 billion. Granted, this sounds like pocket change by today's standards of profligacy. But it was enacted under a Republican government and created a climate of spending that made today's future-sapping expenditures somehow seem acceptable.[40]

Under the Republicans, Americans became aware of the infamous "earmarks." These are spending commitments silently inserted into legislation redistributive favors to a politician's district or a bone thrown to an important contributor. Republican legislators passed spending bills containing tens of thousands of earmarks. At the instigation of individual congressional representatives, funding was provided for thousands of local projects: a film festival here, sidewalk repairs there. It all added up to billions of taxpayer dollars on such projects.[41]

And then, there's good old-fashioned government pork and outright corruption with public money. Think of Alaska's Ted

Stevens, the seven-term Republican senator responsible for the notorious "bridge to nowhere."

Republicans, who once counted spending discipline as a core value, have been as responsible as Democrats for the growth of government in recent years. "We honed the process," one GOP member of the House even admitted about abusive spending during the time when Republicans were in the majority in Congress.[42]

The sad truth is that the 30 percent coalition did not start governing this country in 2008. They've been in charge for years. The only difference is that the Democrats in office today are true believers in the values of the 30 percent coalition.

The real game changer—the opportunity to expand the 30 percent coalition—was not the Democratic sweep in 2008. It was the financial crisis of 2008–2009, which was used as a tool to attack the free-enterprise system and change America's culture for good. It is to that crisis that we now turn.

CHAPTER TWO

A Bill of Goods: The 30 Percent Coalition's Story of the Financial Crisis

A MERICA is a 70–30 nation in favor of free enterprise. Yet the 30 percent coalition is in charge.

This is a puzzle. If free enterprise is so dominant in America, how do we explain the 2008 election? How did the 30 percent coalition decisively take over the White House and leadership of both houses of Congress? One answer is that the Republican brand was in terrible shape, and Republicans have not clearly represented the 70 percent majority for some time. But that isn't the fundamental cause of such an important political change.

The real answer is the economic crisis of 2008–2009.

Many political analysts will tell you that the 2008 election reflected an authentic shift to the left in America's political ideology. But they are wrong. The data are clear: The outcome of the election was primarily due to one factor—the state of the economy.

Consider the evidence from the Iowa Electronic Markets (IEM). The IEM is a place to bet on elections—sort of like a political dog race—operated by the business school faculty at the University of Iowa. Participants wager on the outcomes of economic and political events. It is one of the most accurate predictors of American elections because it pools the wisdom of many thousands of people.[1]

The IEM shows that Barack Obama won because of the crisis. The bettors' prediction of an Obama victory was roughly 55 percent in early September, before the big bailouts began. Once the banks crashed in late September, the predicted probability of an Obama win had skyrocketed to 70 percent. By election day it was up to 90 percent.

When the economy melted down, so did the Republican Party's presidential candidate, John McCain. Barack Obama took 53 percent of the popular vote (and 68 percent of the electoral vote), a larger percentage than any winner of a presidential race in decades.[2]

But for the 30 percent coalition, the economic crisis represented more than just a chance to win an election. It was a once-in-a-generation chance to transform American culture. White House chief of staff Rahm Emanuel summed it up best: "Never let a serious crisis go to waste. What I mean by that is it's an opportunity to do things you couldn't do before." The economic crisis presented a golden opportunity for the 30 percent coalition to remake America in its own image. This chapter tells the story of the financial crisis—and how the 30 percent coalition intended to use it to change America's free-enterprise culture for good.[3]

The story of the financial crisis begins in the summer of 2008. At that time, most Americans were enjoying a number of convenient illusions. The economy was sluggish, but we were convinced that America was experiencing a "contained recession." We believed that housing markets might drop in some parts of the country but could never fall nationwide. And we thought that, given everything we knew about good macroeconomic policy, unemployment would not climb above 6 percent.[4]

At a news conference on April 22, 2008, President George Bush had stated, "We're not in a recession; we're in a slowdown." Through the spring and summer months, this remained the party line. John McCain continually referred to an economy that was simply "slowing." And on July 9 one of his top economic advisors dismissed the sluggishness in the economy as nothing more than "a mental recession."[5]

By the end of the summer, of course, all of these assumptions had proved dead wrong. By September 2008, home prices were in free fall nationwide. Foreclosures exploded, infecting banks with toxic loans. Major financial institutions failed, as did firms that insured the value of investments through "credit default swaps" and "collateralized debt obligations"—once-esoteric terms, Americans were now forced to confront in the daily news cycle.

By September, the financial system as a whole appeared ready to collapse. The investment giant Lehman Brothers filed the largest bankruptcy in American history. The Federal Reserve encouraged Bank of America's purchase of troubled Merrill Lynch and seized control of the insurance giant AIG. The U.S. government placed into conservatorship the government-backed mortgage giants, the Federal National Mortgage Association (Fannie Mae) and the Federal Home Loan Mortgage Corporation (Freddie Mac).

Expectations for a contained recession vanished. Americans panicked as the U.S. economy went into a downward spiral, with one market contaminating the next. From the beginning of September 2008 to a week before the election in November, the Dow Jones Stock Index plummeted almost 30 percent.[6]

Americans were getting poorer, and there was no end in sight. Disposable personal income in America dropped at an annualized rate of 8.5 percent in the third quarter of 2008, the largest quarterly decline in the postwar era. Between December 2006 and November 2008, the unemployment rate climbed from 4.4 percent to 6.9 percent and was accelerating. And around the world, at least $50 trillion in household wealth was in the process of being wiped out—equivalent to approximately 100 percent of total world income for one year.[7]

Imagine you bought a home in June 2006 for $400,000. It was likely worth about $293,000 after the election of 2008—and much less in places like California or Florida. Millions of Americans simply "turned in their keys": As their houses became less valuable than what they owed on their mortgages, they chose the route of home foreclosure.[8]

In the fall of 2008 the outgoing president, George W. Bush, tried to put a brave face on what was clearly an awful situation. "I'm confident," he said, "that our capital markets are flexible and resilient and can deal with these adjustments." And on September 17, President Bush's Treasury secretary Henry Paulson told the nation, "There is a reasonable chance that the biggest part of the housing correction can be behind us in a number of months." It turns out Paulson was right. It was just a *large* number of months.[9]

The public responded by handing the American economy over to the Democrats. In November 2008, they voted Barack Obama into the White House and gave the Democrats majorities in both houses of Congress. Democrats interpreted this as an endorsement of a type of fiscal liberalism not seen since the days of Jimmy Carter. They came into office armed with plans to bail out and stimulate the economy to the tune of trillions. When Republican congressional leaders objected to the scale of the spending, the new president sought to silence them with two words of fact: "I won."[10]

Across the country, those who complained or urged restraint were marginalized. They were branded as little more than opportunists and obstructionists, champions of the discredited policies of the past. Any delay in passing the new spending programs, the newly empowered Democrats argued, might prevent the United States from *ever* recovering from the economic crisis.

The White House and the new Congress believed Americans would swallow any amount of spending they proposed.

This included shoring up distressed bank assets, stimulating various moribund parts of the economy, bailing out uncompetitive companies, and rewarding homeowners who found their underwater mortgages to be a lousy investment.

The mainstream press cheered the process with a stream of shameless puff pieces on the new president and uncritical coverage of his plans. A January 28 *New York Times* editorial lauded the stimulus bill as a "signature achievement" for the new government. "President Obama and the lawmakers who wrote the bill are to be commended," it went on. "Republicans' objections are mostly ideological." The following week, the same editorial pages declared, "We're happy to see President Obama getting tough with congressional Republicans who are trying to sabotage the stimulus and recovery bill and bring even greater ruin on the economy."[11]

By the end of March 2009, the U.S. government and the Federal Reserve had spent, lent, or pledged some $12.8 trillion of America's future prosperity. It was an enormous amount, rivaling the value of everything produced in the U.S. economy in 2008. Put another way, it was enough to buy 88 percent of the value of all the mortgages in America.[12]

"We Are All Socialists Now," the cover of *Newsweek* told Americans. "In many ways our economy already resembles a European one," the magazine concluded. "As boomers age and spending grows, we will become even more French." By "more French" *Newsweek* did not mean baguettes and nice wine. They meant the France of big bureaucracies, powerful labor unions, punitive taxes, high unemployment, and a burgeoning public sector.[13]

Ironically, the leaders of governments in Europe objected to our nation's fiscal bender. At an address to the European Parliament in Strasbourg, the Czech prime minister and European Union president Mirek Topolanek called U.S. deficit spending a "road to hell." Even the communist Chinese became critics of America's profligacy. In January China's Prime Minister Wen Jiabao expressed concern over the way America's ballooning debt might affect the value of Chinese investments in American Treasury bonds. "We have lent a huge amount of money to the U.S.," said the prime minister. "Of course we are concerned about the safety of our assets. To be honest, I am definitely a little worried."[14]

The financial meltdown explains the left's victory. But why? The answer is *not* that the Democrats were willing to spend their way out of the crisis while the Republicans had been tight-fisted. Republican complaints about the new government's overspending were legitimate, but more than a little hypocritical. After all, for years congressional Republicans had been spending like, well, congressmen. And Republicans' first reaction to the financial crisis was to spend as much money as possible. Indeed, it was a Republican administration that offered up the notorious Troubled Asset Relief Program (TARP). With a total price tag of $700 billion, TARP was signed into law in October 2008.[15]

Republicans bailed out the auto industry as well. General Motors and Chrysler, which for years had set themselves up to fail through poor management and toadying to rapacious labor unions, were completely bankrupt. But they argued, in the finest style of any third-world state industry, that they were too big to fail. The government agreed, and in December 2008 the companies received an early Christmas present of $17.4 billion.[16]

So Republicans spent with abandon, and Democrats went on to spend even more. Spending per se wasn't the real difference between the Republicans and the Democrats for voters. The difference was that the Republicans had no compelling explanation for the crisis, seemed responsible for it, and had no obvious plans to fix it.

Meanwhile, the 30 percent coalition offered a full story. Ordinary Americans were not to blame for the financial crisis, nor was government. The real culprits were Wall Street and the Bush administration, which had gutted the regulatory system that was supposed to keep the banks in line. The solution was obvious: Vote for politicians who would hit the brakes on free markets and grow the government in such a way as to regulate the dangerous excesses of capitalism. And most importantly, the middle class would not bear the burden of the costs this growth would entail. Only the very wealthy would be affected.

It was a compelling narrative for a lot of Americans who were in a temporary panic. Billionaire investment bankers certainly didn't inspire any compassion. And Republicans seemed out of touch and unprincipled. Many Americans were willing to believe that the public bore none of the blame for the crisis. For many, the prospect of a big paternalistic government rescuing the nation from crisis seemed appealing as stock markets and home prices spiraled ever downwards. *Regime change* was an obvious, and easy, answer for enough voters to sweep the Democrats to victory.

Unfortunately for America, the 30 percent coalition's narrative was wrong on every point. The truth is that the government started and fueled the crisis. Politicians at fault profited from it and prevaricated to avoid blame. Along with the government, a small percentage of accomplices on Main Street and Wall Street were rewarded for irresponsible and unethical behavior, holding the rest of us hostage. And the American middle class is going to pay dearly for it.

If we continue to accept the prevailing narrative, it will have permanent consequences for our culture of freedom, individual opportunity, and entrepreneurship.

The 30 percent's narrative about the financial crisis consists of five key claims:

- Government was not the primary cause of the economic crisis.
- The government understands the crisis and knows how to fix it.
- Main Street Americans were nothing more than victims of the crisis.
- The only way to save the economy is through massive government growth and deficit spending.
- The middle class will not pay for the stimulus package. Only the rich will.

All of these claims are false. To get the real story of the financial crisis, we need to dismantle this narrative piece by piece.

Government Was Not the Primary Cause of the Economic Crisis

All throughout the crisis, politicians in Washington have emphasized the role of private sector greed in bringing about the financial collapse. But in point of fact, the economic crisis was caused in large part by the government itself.[17]

The government's failure is most blatant in the implosion of Fannie Mae and Freddie Mac. Through these two government-sponsored enterprises (GSEs), politicians pulled off some of their most dramatic, and costly, efforts at social engineering. At the same time, they enriched their political campaigns. And in the process, they perverted the most basic rules of the free-enterprise system.

Fannie and Freddie are in the home mortgage business. Neither is a government agency, but both have government backing in case of failure. They don't make loans directly. The principal activity of both corporations is to purchase mortgage loans from the banks that issue (or "originate") them, bundle these loans into investments called mortgage-backed securities (MBSs), and then hold these securities or sell them to investors.[18]

Over the years, the government has used Fannie and Freddie as tools of social engineering. Both institutions had "affordable housing" quotas. Government regulators gave the two institutions a clear mandate: expand home ownership by increasing the level of lending to low-income homebuyers. Why expand home ownership, you might ask? The reason isn't ridiculous on its face: Homeowners tend to be better citizens and neighbors than nonhomeowners. (There's a reason most people don't want to live next door to a rented house.)

The trouble is that the government never knows when enough is enough. If home ownership is good, more is always and everywhere better. Congress and the White House pushed Fannie and Freddie in the 1990s to buy up more and more loans made to riskier and riskier mortgage borrowers. If you couldn't get a loan, the Clinton administration believed, it might be evidence not simply of bad credit, but of something more sinister: discrimination. This is typical statist thinking, of course: Private markets are never just. They are always a ruse for hurting the vulnerable and helping the powerful—and government always needs to fix the problem.[19]

Fannie and Freddie were used by the government to stimulate more loans to people who had bad credit. They did this by announcing their intention to buy these loans if banks and mortgage companies would originate them. Basically, it was like the government telling banks to make lousy loans and then taking these loans off the banks' hands for more than they were really worth. Later, they were shocked—*shocked!*—to learn that banks were making overly risky loans.

As a result, the two housing GSEs began to hold millions of nontraditional (junk) loans that would ultimately cause Fannie and Freddie to fail. Many of these were so-called subprime and

Alt-A mortgages, which are basically loans to people who shouldn't get loans. Think of it this way: If you put down 20 percent on a house and have good credit, you almost certainly have a "prime" mortgage. But if you have low credit scores or no down payment—in other words, if it is not sensible to lend you money—you probably have a subprime or Alt-A mortgage.[20]

By 1997, Fannie Mae was stimulating and buying subprime and Alt-A loans secured with nothing more than a 3 percent down payment. Four years later (by this time under the Bush administration), it was buying mortgages with no down payment at all. But even this was still not enough for Washington's social engineers. "Make more risky loans," said Congress. New government mandates required Fannie and Freddie to increase their low- and moderate-income loans to at least 55 percent of their mortgage purchases. From 2001 to 2006, subprime loans rose from 7 percent to nearly 19 percent of all new mortgages and Alt-As from just over 2 percent to nearly 14 percent.[21]

In the early part of this decade, you probably became aware that it was suspiciously easy to buy a new house. Maybe you even commented on the fact that an irresponsible friend or relative had gotten a loan he didn't deserve and couldn't afford. Between 2005 and 2007, Fannie and Freddie bought $1 trillion in Alt-A and subprime mortgages. More than 61 percent of Freddie's purchases in those years were of mortgages to statistically uncreditworthy borrowers. Some 62 percent of Fannie's loans and 58 percent of Freddie's required down payments of less than 10 percent.[22]

At the same time, the Federal Reserve was pursuing a super-low interest rate policy that pushed down mortgage rates and seemed to make home-ownership more affordable. Americans who would otherwise have rented a house or an apartment now bought more house than they could afford, and with little or nothing down. Home prices began to rise precipitously from the increased demand, and the now-famous housing bubble quickly inflated. Without Fannie and Freddie—and without a little push from our government—this would not have happened. Banks and investors aren't in the business of losing money by lending to people who are unlikely to pay them back.[23]

Predictably, when house prices stopped rising and mortgage payments had to be made, people began to default. Those holding subprime mortgages defaulted at ten times the rate of those who held prime mortgages. Anybody surprised by this was either willfully ignorant (many congressmen) or was unable to follow what was really going on (most of the general public).[24]

Before bursting, the bubble promoted by the government infected the whole housing market. The Fed kept interest rates low. Private firms rushed to compete in the secondhand mortgage market with Fannie and Freddie. And banks made more and more high-risk loans. As a result, house prices increased by double digits in cities all over the country. For years house prices rose and never fell. And as tends to happen in such circumstances, people began to believe that a bubble was not a bubble but real value. Housing professionals even argued the absurd—that housing prices *could not* fall nationwide.

If this was true, then investing in real estate was a surefire bet, and no amount of leverage was too risky. International banks and investment firms began buying MBSs, largely on credit. They borrowed many times more money than their capital—as much as 30 times more—and spent the money on MBSs. This was no problem, of course, if house prices kept rising and MBSs continued to perform. But it was a big problem when house prices fell, people defaulted on their mortgages, and the value of MBSs dropped.[25]

To illustrate, say you are an investment firm with $1 million in capital. You borrow $30 million and plow it into MBSs. In the good times, the highly leveraged MBSs yield extraordinarily high returns and you don't have to cut into your capital to pay back your loans. But when the housing bubble starts to burst, the opposite happens, and it takes next to nothing to wipe you out. Just a few percentage points downward in the value of MBSs means you owe more than the value of your capital, and you are bankrupt. This is the essence of the Wall Street meltdown. It is what crushed Merrill Lynch, Bear Sterns, Citigroup, and Lehman Brothers.[26]

Was it just bad luck? No, it was bad judgment and greed. According to legendary financier and free-market advocate Carl Icahn, "Wall Street firms went out and securitized mortgages—that was how it all started. . . . It was taking undue risk." Why did they do this? Icahn is uncensored in his views about Wall Street leadership. "These CEOs, with many exceptions, are very mediocre guys."[27]

But don't forget the root of the problem: Fannie and Freddie. These government-sponsored companies and their enablers in Congress sparked the fire that burned down our financial system.

It's bad enough that politicians focus on Wall Street's role in the crisis instead of their own. But it's even more galling that many congressmen—perhaps *your* congressman—actually profited from Fannie and Freddie's sins.

Congress was well warned of the risks that Fannie and Freddie were creating. In 2005 Federal Reserve chairman Alan Greenspan warned Congress that action was needed on the GSEs. Unchecked, Fannie and Freddie would "create ever-growing potential systemic risk down the road," he said. "We are placing the total financial system of the future at a substantial risk." In response to Greenspan's warnings, the Senate Banking Committee passed a serious Fannie and Freddie reform bill in 2005. The bill required both companies to eliminate their investments in risky assets, but it was never made into law. It was killed in the full Senate.[28]

One who helped kill the bill was Connecticut's senator Christopher Dodd. This shouldn't surprise anyone, though—the powerful chairman of the Senate Banking Committee had received more in campaign contributions from employees and political action committees at Fannie and Freddie than any other senator ($165,000).

Contributions from Fannie and Freddie were not limited to Senate Democrats, however. Dodd was in good company among

Republicans and Democrats alike and in both the Senate and the House. Fannie and Freddie had friends all over Capitol Hill. So in the end, little was done about the GSEs—until September 2008, that is, when they melted down and were bailed out.[29]

How much has all this cost you, the taxpayer? By November 2009, the Federal Reserve had purchased $700 billion of mortgage-backed securities from Fannie and Freddie. And the U.S. Treasury secretary stated that the government would provide "unlimited" funds to support Fannie and Freddie over the next two years.[30]

But the politicians never seem to learn—or at least they hope the voters never catch on. Despite catastrophic losses, the government is in the process of expanding Fannie and Freddie once again. With help from the Treasury and the Fed, Fannie and Freddie not only own or guarantee more than half of all mortgages used to buy homes, but they are now expanding their operations to help independent mortgage banks get funding for making new home loans. After all, that's the only way some people will be able to buy a house, right? And home ownership is a good thing, right? And so off we go again.[31]

The government was the principal cause of the crisis. Yet we allowed our elected leaders to cover their tracks, blame others, and profit personally. Indeed, so confident were they that we wouldn't figure out the truth that they offered us an enlarged government as the *solution* to the problems they created.

According to the narrative of the 30 percent coalition, government was at fault in *one* way: It wasn't big enough under Bush. Over and over again, they claimed that the meltdown was due to the lack of government oversight and insufficient financial regulation. If only there had been more regulators watching the banks more closely, the economy wouldn't have collapsed.

There is little evidence to support this argument. The data point in exactly the opposite direction. In fact, regulatory spending and staffing actually rose faster during the Bush administration than during the Clinton administration. One study shows that the costs of social and economic regulation skyrocketed by an amazing 60 percent under Bush—compared to 8 percent during Clinton's first term and 21 percent during his second.[32]

And here's the most inconvenient fact of all: The financial sector—where the financial crisis began and where it had the most serious impact—was *not* deregulated during the Bush years. In fact, the most heavily regulated institutions in the financial system—commercial banks—were at the very center of the crisis. The crisis happened *despite* an extensive, intrusive regulatory framework, not because the framework didn't exist.

So there was no lack of financial regulation under Bush. But what if there had been even more regulation—1940s-style limits on banking and financial firms—as the 30 percent coalition favors? The answer is that nothing would have changed. Regulation is useless if regulators cannot understand the risks at hand or catch bad behavior. And apparently, they *can't* catch bad behavior—not even overt fraud about which they were repeatedly warned. Case in point: Bernard Madoff.

The infamous Bernie Madoff was the head of a respected Wall Street investment firm. He was well connected in the industry and in Washington, and at one time was chairman of the NASDAQ stock exchange. But Madoff's principal product, a multibillion-dollar investment fund, turned out to be nothing more than a massive Ponzi scheme. Over the years, the financier systematically defrauded thousands of investors of billions of dollars, from corporate clients and foundations to individuals who had entrusted to him their life savings. Madoff's victims included a number of charities, among them the Women's Zionist Organization of America and Steven Spielberg's Wunderkinder Foundation. A charity established by Holocaust survivor and writer Elie Wiesel was wiped out in the fraud.[33]

For years a federal whistleblower had tried to alert the Securities and Exchange Commission (SEC) to Madoff's scheme. The whistleblower detailed his findings for investigators, but they failed to uncover any wrongdoing. "They had every red flag in the world," says a lawyer for Madoff's victims. "Even with a map and a flashlight, they couldn't find it."[34]

In the aftermath of the scandal, SEC officials were called to a hearing before the House Financial Services subcommittee. The February 2009 hearing was a contentious affair, perhaps the worst day in the agency's history. The SEC was accused of relying on bureaucrats and lawyers who did not understand the complexity of the markets. "You couldn't find your backside with two hands if the lights were on," New York Democratic congressman Gary Ackerman told them. "You have totally and thoroughly failed in your mission." He concluded, "We thought the enemy was Mr. Madoff. I think it was you."[35]

The congressman's point was well taken—although some-what ironic. After all, Congressman Ackerman was a member of the Financial Services Committee that presided as the American financial system melted down and was put on welfare. And the solution of congressmen such as Mr. Ackerman? More government, with enhanced regulatory powers.

In June 2009 President Obama put forward his plan for what those regulatory powers should be. The plan charged the Federal Reserve with regulating risk across the entire financial system and creating a Financial Services Oversight Council to identify financial firms "whose combination of size, leverage, and interconnectedness could pose a threat to financial stability if they failed." The plan also included the creation of a new "consumer financial protection agency," heightened capital requirements for banks, and strengthened international financial regulations.[36]

In short, the 30 percent coalition gave us more regulation and bureaucracy. But more government does not mean we will be safe. On the contrary, it will most likely give us a false sense of security, especially when a primary culprit in the crisis is the government that creates the new rules and carries them out.

The Government Understands the Crisis and Knows How to Fix It

After winning the election, President Obama surrounded himself with some of the top economists in the country. He had to if he wanted the public to believe the second component of the

30 percent's story about the economic meltdown: The government understands the financial crisis and can solve it with aggressive action.

In fact, most government officials—liberal and conservative—do not understand the crisis and do not know how to fix it. The economy is unbelievably complicated. Many people have told me they find the current crisis utterly incomprehensible. They are impressed by the economists who understand what's going on and trust them more or less like they trust their doctors. The doctor says, "Take this pill," and you take it. Government officials say, "I'm spending a trillion dollars on yo-yos," and you're supposed to assume that yo-yos are terrific for the economy.

The trust in economic officials is misplaced. There is little evidence that the people guiding our economy understand the dynamics of the current crisis well enough to fix it. After all, very few of them predicted that there was any kind of problem at hand—not even close. As Vice President Joe Biden put it, "We and everyone else misread the economy." Federal Reserve economists were still forecasting significant positive growth and moderate unemployment in May and June 2008. They believed that economic growth in 2009 would be 2.4 percent, and unemployment would be 5.5 percent. What we experienced instead was negative growth, double-digit unemployment, and the destruction of at least $50 trillion in worldwide wealth. No one can get the numbers exactly right, of course. But getting them this much wrong certainly lends a whole new meaning to the expression "margin of error."[37]

To be fair, it's not just government economists who can't forecast worth a hill of beans. A May 2008 Bloomberg survey of professional economists (both in and out of government) found that the average growth projection for 2009 was 2 percent. Projected unemployment was 5.3 percent. Virtually the only economists correctly predicting the recession were the same economists who have been predicting economic doom for 15 years—the proverbial stopped watches that are right twice a day.[38]

Even if they don't know what works to fix the economy, politicians should now have a sense of what *doesn't* work—namely, the policies that led us to disaster in the first place. In the spirit of "do no harm," you might expect our representatives to desist from the social engineering that stimulated so much irresponsible behavior. Your expectations would be misplaced. The government is back at work, cooking up more schemes that will lead to waste and abuse with your money.

Witness the now-infamous "Cash for Clunkers" program launched in July 2009. The $1 billion program was designed to encourage Americans to trade in their older cars for new, more fuel-efficient vehicles by offering them a taxpayer subsidy of up to $4,500. This was billed as an attempt to simultaneously stimulate auto-buying and lower energy consumption. But it was really a program to reward a favored industry. Remember, the government is now in the car business since the GM and Chrysler bailouts.

A flier mailed out to potential customers by one Chevrolet dealer in Virginia tells the story best.

Bad Credit? No Credit? Bankruptcy? Divorce? Charge-offs?
For the Next 4 Days We Are Guaranteeing Credit Approval!
Virginia Banks Ordered to Lend Money Now! No Overnight
Camping.

The dealer's expectations proved justified. The $1 billion
appropriated for the program, which was supposed to run
through November, was gone by the end of July. But more
money was forthcoming—there's always more money—and Congress quickly allocated an additional $2 billion.[39]

There is no evidence that the billions spent in the Cash for
Clunkers program created more than an economic hiccup in the
third quarter of 2009, and nothing lasting. Worse, many economists believe it will have a long-term negative impact on our
economy if it crowds out other consumer expenditures later on.[40]

Another government invitation to abuse was the "First-Time
Homebuyer Credit." Through this program Congress offered
those who purchased a home for the first time in 2008 or 2009
a tax credit of up to $8,000. The fact that you had not actually
purchased a home during those years did not seem to be an
insurmountable obstacle. Just by claiming you had, the IRS
would mail you a check.

This program not only invited homebuyer fraud, it also provided no way for the government to investigate that fraud. As the
IRS deputy commissioner later testified before the House Ways
and Means Committee, "The statute did not grant the IRS the
authority to disallow claims based on insufficient documentation." Why? Because, continued the IRS official, "Requiring

paper documentation up front with the tax return would have caused all taxpayers claiming the credit to wait longer." In other words, insisting on proof would have slowed the spending.[41]

As a result—surprise, surprise—the U.S. Treasury Inspector General for Tax Administration found that nearly 74,000 individuals who *already owned a home* claimed the First-Time Homebuyer Credit. And more than 19,300 claims were made by those who had never bought a home at all. The youngest of the "taxpayers" to receive the credit were 4 years old.[42]

The truth is that the government did not learn from its mistakes. Even at the bottom of the hole, it continued to dig.

Main Street Americans Were Nothing More Than Victims of the Crisis

The fraud in the First-Time Homebuyer Credit program might tip you off that American homeowners aren't always entirely virtuous. They might even deserve a little blame in the mortgage crisis. Yet a central aspect of the 30 percent coalition's narrative of the economic crisis is that ordinary American citizens are merely *victims* of avaricious bankers and predatory mortgage lenders. According to Barney Frank, the powerful chairman of the House Financial Services Committee during the 111th Congress, people who foreclosed on their homes in the mortgage crisis "were misled, were deceived or were in other ways the victims of unfair lending practices." It's a comforting, populist message, but also an alarmingly pernicious one that dispenses entirely with any respect for personal accountability.[43]

Consider a real-life home foreclosure story: the case of Edmund Andrews, an economics reporter with the *New York Times*. Andrews was a finance-savvy man who had covered the dot-com collapse in 2000 and the Asian financial crisis three years before that. He does not fit the profile of a poor, ignorant victim. But as he put it in a *New York Times* article, "In 2004 I joined millions of otherwise-sane Americans in what we now know was a catastrophic binge." The binge in question was real estate that he could not afford, purchased with borrowed money he could not repay.

Everyone seemed to be getting easy credit. So Andrews and his wife decided to do the same. And they were stunned at just how much money they could get their hands on. Andrews summed up his mortgage broker's attitude this way: "Who am I to tell you that you shouldn't do what you want to do? I am here to sell money and to help you do what you want to do." Because his credit was good, Andrews was able to stretch his finances beyond what his income could justify. The mortgage he signed had a lower rate for the first five years and a higher rate for the next 25. But house prices were rising. And in five years' time he felt confident he would be able to refinance before the higher rates kicked in.[44]

Things would not turn out that way, however. Within the year, Andrews and his wife had started to run up more credit card debt than they could handle. Eventually, they took out a subprime loan. This allowed them to pay off their credit cards, but soon they were even deeper in debt. They couldn't make their monthly mortgage payments. Foreclosure and bankruptcy loomed. What's more, this wasn't the first bankruptcy in the Andrews family. His wife had gone bankrupt twice before.[45]

So who is at fault here? Mortgage brokers may have been too eager to lend, and their standards had been corrupted by Fannie and Freddie. But many borrowers, far from being victims, were often too ready to take loans they shouldn't have, chasing the lure of easy profits on rising house prices.

The data show an amazing pattern of malfeasance and irresponsibility by millions of American homebuyers. One study found that in the run-up to the crash, up to 70 percent of early mortgage defaulters (people who defaulted in the first three months of their mortgages) had made fraudulent representations on their original loan applications. They lied, went bankrupt, and walked away from their debt.[46]

And many people who walked away from their mortgages didn't have to. Economists call this "strategic foreclosure" and have estimated that at least a quarter of foreclosers were perfectly able to stay in their homes but elected not to simply because those homes had turned out to be a bad deal.[47]

In the summer of 2009, more than one-fifth of U.S. mortgage-holders were "underwater": They owed more than their homes were worth. This was due to three things. First, the price of their homes fell during the housing bust. Second, their down payment was too low. And third, many had refinanced to take out the equity they had built up, effectively using their homes as ATM machines.[48]

Many walked away because they could do so at relatively low personal cost. In most parts of the United States, unlike in other countries, home loans are "nonrecourse": If you default on your loan, the bank can take your house but can't take your other assets to cover what you owe. It is shockingly easy to stick someone else with the bill for an investment that you made— and one you made with little or none of your own money.[49]

The evidence shows that for many people, strategic foreclosure during the housing crisis depended primarily on personal ethics—or a lack thereof. Using data on foreclosures from 2008 and 2009, economists have found that people who consider it immoral to default on their mortgages are 77 percent less likely to do so than people who don't think it is immoral. Foreclosure also depends on what seems like "normal" behavior. Data show that even correcting for their financial circumstances, people who know someone who defaulted are 82 percent more likely to do so themselves than if they don't have any acquaintances foreclosing.[50]

Yet through 2009, the administration clung to the claim that people were foreclosing on their mortgages only because they had no choice. In other words, personal accountability was not the problem. In a bailout for foreclosing homeowners, the administration lowered the payments of hundreds of thousands of "at-risk" mortgage holders to a maximum of 31 percent of household income. Government and the banks would pick up the rest of the tab.[51]

The program was a disaster. About half of all such restructured mortgages went back into default within six months because government has steadfastly refused to face the truth: The problem in many cases was not the size of the monthly house payment but the attitudes of those making the payments. Some foreclosers had no option, of course. But millions of mortgage defaulters were people who simply walked away from mortgages they considered a bad investment.[52]

Until recently, losing one's home was considered the worst financial calamity that could befall a person. In the 30 percent coalition's America, voluntary foreclosure is being embraced as a practical financial option. An actual company called You Walk Away is evidence of this: "Are you stressed out about mortgage payments? Is foreclosure right for you?" In response to these questions, the company's website was getting some 25,000 hits daily in February 2009. For a fee of $995, the company promised to do the following: stop lenders from harassing you, put you in touch with lawyers and accountants, and show you how to "stay in your home for up to 8 months or more without having to pay anything to your lender."[53]

The 30 percent coalition's fiction about the innocence of homeowners was almost as pernicious as its fiction about the innocence of government. Ignoring the role of Main Street encourages more abuses in the future. Worse yet, it is deeply unfair to the more than nine in ten Americans who did not foreclose on a mortgage—including the majority of those who found themselves underwater but stayed in their homes and paid their mortgages anyway. Once again, the 30 percent coalition is rewarding the takers in America and penalizing the makers.[54]

The Only Way to Save the Economy Is Through Massive Government Growth and Deficit Spending

"This recession might linger for years," President Obama warned us during his first full month in office. "Our nation will sink deeper into a crisis that, at some point, we may not be able to reverse."[55]

Having spelled out the problem, the new president then went on to outline the solution. "At this particular moment, only government can provide the short-term boost necessary to lift us from a recession this deep and severe," Obama told us. "Only government can break the vicious cycles that are crippling our economy." Eleven months later, he said that we must continue to "spend our way out of this recession."[56]

The most expensive aspect of the government's narrative of the economic crisis is that without massive spending, the economy might never recover.

Expensive and false. First, recessions can and do end without stimulus. Since the mid-1850s, the average length of recessions is about 17 months. There are, of course, different views as to how long the current recession will last and how severe it will prove to be. But whether the U.S. economy develops according to the best-case scenario or according to the worst, one thing is certain: The current recession will end. All serious economists accept the truth of this statement. (Equally true, unfortunately, is the fact that this will not be the last recession.)[57]

Second, attempts to shore up the economy with massive public spending have done little to improve matters and have served primarily to chain future generations with debt. At a cost of more than $2,500 per American, the stimulus package has spectacularly overpromised and underdelivered.

Take the case of unemployment. The administration's expectations about the impact of the stimulus package on unemployment were grossly inflated. According to White House economists in January 2009, the government's recovery plan would keep the unemployment rate below 8 percent. Without the stimulus, they argued, unemployment would rise to between 8 and 9 percent.

This was wrong on both counts. The impotence of the stimulus spending is indicated by the fact that by October 2009 unemployment had risen to 10.2 percent and was still hovering near 10 percent in spring of 2010.[58]

Ten percent unemployment is not much to be proud of. In the face of this failure, the government has turned to spinning the data. Sure, they say, many parts of the economy are getting crushed, such as construction and manufacturing. Lots of people in those industries are out of work and suffering. But some parts of the economy, the administration points out, are performing relatively well. Government data even show that a couple of industries in January 2010 had unemployment below 6 percent.[59]

But look closely at these industries: They are *government* and *unpaid work*. In other words, the administration is pleased to report that in today's economy, bureaucrats and volunteers are doing just fine. That's quite some consolation.

The fact is, the stimulus package has been a remarkable failure when it comes to creating new jobs. The administration claims that the stimulus spending created or saved 640,329 jobs by the last quarter of 2009. Given the $275 billion from the stimulus devoted to programs to create jobs, that means every new job costs the American taxpayer $429,000. According to Census Bureau numbers, in 2008 the median wage for full-time jobs was $37,115. With benefits, let's round this up generously to $50,000. If the stimulus money were being spent as efficiently as private-sector money is, the stimulus should have created nearly 5.5 million jobs.[60]

The administration responded to such criticisms by noting that the stimulus hadn't all been spent. Many "shovel-ready" projects were still tied up in administrative red tape. By the last quarter of 2009, for example, the departments of Defense, Energy, Homeland Security, Interior, and Transportation had spent less than a quarter of their allocated stimulus funds. By January of 2010 only a third of the total funds had been paid out, with a fraction of that having been actually spent on completed projects. The president's budget director admitted to Congress that "even those [public works] that are 'on the shelf' generally cannot be undertaken quickly enough to provide timely stimulus to the economy."[61]

In other words, the stimulus will hit the budget too late to help the economy out of the crisis—perhaps just in time to stimulate inflation instead. This is reason enough to say it is a failed policy. But there are additional reasons why the stimulus can be considered a bust.

To begin with, there is little evidence that stimulus spending actually returns as much as it spends. A September 2009 study published by the National Bureau of Economic Research argues that federal spending programs in America have generally raised GDP by *less than* they cost. The most effective part of any stimulus package is not spending, but tax reductions. Research shows that lowering taxes *does* spur the economy—by increasing disposable incomes, consumer demand, and incentives and rewards for work—and thereby raises real GDP. Unfortunately, of the $200 billion of tax relief in the stimulus package, only $88 billion were allocated during 2009, when relief was most needed.[62]

So where does the stimulus spending stimulate? The answer is that much of it goes to pork-barrel projects and social engineering. Some $400 million has gone to global warming research and over $1.5 billion to carbon-capture demonstration projects. The arts has gotten its share: $50 million has been allocated to the National Endowment for the Arts and $25 million to the Smithsonian Institution. Although these may be good things, such spending hardly seems the most efficient way to stimulate the economy. Indeed, many projects have hardly even a patina of economic stimulus, such as the $886,000 for an "environmentally and financially sustainable" Frisbee golf course in Austin, Texas.[63]

Stimulus also opens the door to fraud. Earl Devaney, who runs the federal government's Recovery Act Accountability and Transparency Board, has conceded that $55 billion or more in stimulus money could be lost to waste and malfeasance.[64]

In short, the stimulus has not been a success despite what politicians say, and was not a clear necessity in the first place.

Opposing the stimulus package was not a disreputable position. Whatever the government tries to tell you, being against the stimulus does not make you a crank, a radical, or a conspiracy theorist.

The Middle Class Will Not Pay for the Stimulus Package—Only the Rich Will

"I can make a firm pledge. Under my plan, no family making less than $250,000 a year will see any form of tax increase. Not your income tax, not your payroll tax, not your capital gains taxes, not any of your taxes." That's what Barack Obama declared on September 12, 2008, in Dover, New Hampshire.[65]

Perhaps the most outrageously disingenuous claim of all in the left's narrative was that the middle class would not pay for the new policies. The argument went like this: Yes, the level of spending may seem to be sheer madness. But don't worry, "the rich" will pay for it. Even better, the middle class will come out ahead if the bailouts and government spending actually turn a profit for the taxpayer.

In truth, *everyone* will pay, including the middle class. And they will pay for what is a terrible "investment." There is no way around this.

Throughout the election and up until the time of writing this book, the president had promised to increase taxes only on the rich—defined as those earning more than $200,000 ($250,000 for couples)—and to cut them for everyone else. In other words, he was claiming that raising the marginal tax rates on America's richest 3 percent alone could provide the revenue to close the country's growing fiscal gap and fund all of the planned new spending.

This claim was implausible. There wouldn't be nearly enough money from simply taxing the rich—even if the rich didn't avoid their rising taxes by working less, investing less, and starting fewer businesses.

Liberal and conservative economists agree that the middle class will have to pay. This is also the consensus among such figures as Stuart Taylor of *National Journal*, the editors of the *Washington Post*, and Clive Crook of *The Atlantic*. As liberal *New York Times* columnist and Nobel economics laureate Paul Krugman admits, "I at least find it hard to see how the federal government can meet its long-term obligations without some tax increases on the middle class."[66]

The inconvenient truth is that the fiscal burden will fall on the middle class, too. The Urban-Brookings Tax Policy Center (a collaboration between two left-leaning think tanks) calculates that the average effective federal tax rate for Americans will jump from 18.2 percent in 2009 to between 20.7 and 23.4 percent in 2012. This will include real tax increases for every income group, from poorest to richest. The biggest reason for this is that as incomes increase, millions of low- and middle-income Americans will be forced into higher tax brackets.[67]

In some cases, the burden will practically all fall on folks who earn less than $200,000. Economist Kevin Hassett illustrates this point with the taxes advocated by Democrats to pay for the health care reforms they proposed in 2009. These taxes were supposed to be levied on so-called Cadillac plans—health insurance plans carried by the well-off that exceed $8,000 in benefits per person or $21,000 per family. The taxes were proposed to pay for the uninsured and discourage overuse of the health care system. Hassett showed that 87 percent of the taxes would actually be paid by those making under $200,000.[68]

The government can *say* the middle and lower classes will not pay for the government's spending spree, but it is not true. The taxes might be obscured, buried, or left to be paid by future taxpayers. The taxes will come, though, and not just to the rich.[69]

The other government claim about the current spending spree is that middle-class taxpayers might ultimately see a positive return on their national "investment." Don't get your hopes up.

In June 2009 President Obama announced that the hugely expensive TARP bailouts had actually begun to turn a profit. This happened when some of the financial institutions started paying back their TARP dollars. But we're getting only a part of the picture here. Yes, the U.S. government will make $3 billion from bailing out the banks. But according to a January 2010 Congressional Budget Office (CBO) report, other programs that received TARP money will result in enormous losses. The Home Affordable Mortgage Program, for example, will end up costing the taxpayers of this country $20 billion.[70]

Still, even a few billion repaid is better than nothing, right?

Not so fast. Congress members Barney Frank, Maxine Waters, Dennis Cardoza, and Nydia Velazquez were working to make sure that the repaid money was directed to people more deserving than you. The original TARP legislation stipulated that any profits would be "paid into the general fund of the

Treasury for reduction of the public debt." But these politicians had their own plans for the money. In 2009 they introduced a bill entitled "TARP for Main Street" that would take repaid money and spend it on a number of housing proposals they have been advocating to fund low-income rental housing and to subsidize mortgage defaulters. In other words, they want to take the money and do more of the kind of thing that created the housing crisis in the first place.[1]

The claim that middle-class taxpayers will benefit from the current policies is simply false. No matter what the president and his colleagues in the 30 percent coalition tell you, it is not just "the rich" who will pay for their epic financial bender. It is *you* and *your children* who will face higher taxes. Furthermore, positive returns on what the government handed out are almost certainly fictional. And politicians have plans to siphon off whatever money is paid back toward even more social engineering schemes.

Misassigned blame, false assertions, and destructive public policy are the true story of the financial crisis and the story that the government's narrative brilliantly obfuscated. The objective was to tell a story about the financial crisis that leveraged it into a game-changer for American culture—to transform a culture of entrepreneurship into one of statism and to make the 30 percent coalition a permanent majority.

Will it work? Maybe. Stories, even untrue ones, are powerful things in politics. They shape thinking and drive public policy. Consider another powerful narrative in American history—the story of the Great Depression.

The conventional wisdom about the Great Depression runs something like this: President Herbert Hoover was an uncritical free-marketeer, and the free markets he championed led to the ruin of the American economy. Only Roosevelt's New Deal government spending and social safety net could save the country from permanent economic destruction.

This story has been seared into our brains from grade school. The problem is, it is wrong.

Herbert Hoover was no free-marketeer. He intervened in free markets with gusto, whether the area was wages (keeping them artificially high) or financing ailing institutions (by creating the Reconstruction Finance Corporation). His biographer Joan Hoff Wilson wrote, "The Hoover administration became the first in American history to use the power of the federal government to intervene directly in the economy in time of peace."[72]

But the claim that Roosevelt's New Deal spending saved the country from the Great Depression is the most egregious falsehood of all. In her bestseller *The Forgotten Man*, author Amity Shlaes takes a hard look at the true effects of the New Deal's wild spending—from sponsoring murals to building dams. She shows that it did not succeed in getting the economy moving again. Rather, it heaped massive burdens on the country that more than offset the benefits of the government programs. In fact, Shlaes demonstrates, federal intervention helped prolong the Great Depression and made it deeper than it would otherwise have been.[73]

Shlaes is not alone in her revision of the conventional wisdom surrounding the Great Depression. A 1935 study by the Brookings Institution backs up her findings. It examined the accomplishments of the National Recovery Administration, one of the first of the New Deal programs, which sought to help workers by setting minimum wages and maximum weekly hours. According to the Brookings study, however, the NRA "on the whole returded recovery."[74]

So what did Roosevelt achieve through his spending programs? For a start, he bought a lot of votes. The New Deal offered, in effect, a massive subsidy to many of his core constituencies. He lavished federal money on political interest groups that were important to the Democratic Party—from union workers to journalists, actors, and artists.

More important, however, Roosevelt changed American culture. He succeeded in shifting America in the direction of other emerging statist economies—despite the fact that this shift was at odds with America's unique and exceptional culture. During the Depression Americans were in a panic, which provided an opportunity to make a cultural change without massive public outrage.

A few leaders saw the ruse, however. When Roosevelt created the Works Progress Administration, a public works program that including everything from road construction to literacy and drama projects, Senator Arthur Vandenberg of Michigan was aghast at the scale of the spending. "Four or five billion worth of lost liberty," he called it.[75]

Some realized that the New Deal changed what it meant to be an American. The president's speechwriter, Ray Moley, was one. Moley was so worried that New Deal programs would strip Americans of their independent heritage that he ended up leaving the White House. "I decided that the administration was not the friend of this average American," Moley later recalled. "The chasm had been widening and I was scared, because something was happening that was inimical to that forgotten man."[76]

In retrospect, Roosevelt succeeded (at least in part), not in fixing the economy, but in weakening our culture of free enterprise. The New Deal paved the way for the Great Society's social programs twenty years later. This created generations of Americans on the dole and a massive expansion of permanent government bureaucracies at the federal, state, and local levels. Thanks to Roosevelt, millions of Americans today feel entitled to the wealth created by others. Millions of Americans are comfortable with the idea that it is the government's job to equalize incomes. Plus, we have government programs that support journalists, activism, and artists.

In short, FDR created today's 30 percent coalition. They want to finish the job by turning themselves into a permanent ruling majority. There was nothing new about their narrative. It was the FDR narrative on steroids, intended to lead to greater statism and political gain.

The 30 percent's narrative is absolutely central to the new American culture war. If we reject it, the 70–30 nation will probably remain strong. If we accept it—and base our nation's policies on it—we will be well on our way to European-style social democracy. America will be, in George H. W. Bush's famous caricature of his opponent Michael Dukakis's view, just "another pleasant country on the UN roll call, somewhere between Albania and Zimbabwe."[77] American exceptionalism will be no different than, in Obama's words, British exceptionalism or Greek exceptionalism.

We will have bigger bureaucracies, bigger labor unions, and bigger state-run corporations. It will be harder to be an entrepreneur because of punitive taxes and regulations. The rewards of success will be expropriated for the sake of attaining greater income equality. America will be less willing to stand up for our national interests, less able to attract the best talent, and have less of a gift to offer to the world.

So what? Who really cares if America is not the undisputed leader in entrepreneurship, in strength, and in individual opportunity to prosper? What difference will it make? There's a wrong answer to these questions and a right answer.

First, the wrong answer: Losing the culture struggle to the 30 percent coalition will make us poorer in money. Of course, strictly speaking this answer isn't incorrect—losing the struggle will make us all poorer. But this is the wrong way to answer the question because it completely misses the most important aspect of the matter. Yes, money is vitally important when your job is on the line or you're trying to pay your bills. But what we are really talking about here is a struggle for the next 100 years of American culture, and that, in an already rich country, is not about the money. If we cannot see that freedom, opportunity, and entrepreneurship are about far more than money, shame on us. We don't deserve to prevail in this fight.[78]

The right answer is this: Losing the new culture war will take too much of the life out of our lives. We might be protected from some economic risk and find a cushy job in the government, but we won't truly flourish. We will abrogate the third unalienable right set out in our own Declaration of Independence: *the pursuit of happiness.*

And it is to the pursuit of happiness that I will now turn.

CHAPTER THREE

Free Enterprise and the
Pursuit of Happiness

C URRENT STATIST POLICIES will put America in debt
for a long time. Their policies will allow the government to
dig into our paychecks, stock portfolios, and estates so it can
redistribute our money to those deemed more deserving.

But the stakes are much higher than mere money. The
main issue in the new American culture war between free
enterprise and statism is not material riches—it is human flourishing. This is a battle about nothing less than our ability to
pursue happiness.

The 30 percent coalition claims that its version of America
will be fairer, better, and more virtuous than America has been
in the past. It believes America will be a happier place if there is
less economic inequality. This became clear to many critics during a campaign stop by Barack Obama in Toledo, Ohio, in
October 2008. Samuel Joseph Wurzelbacher ("Joe the Plumber")
asked Mr. Obama, "I'm getting ready to buy a company that

makes 250 to 280 thousand dollars a year. Your new tax plan is going to tax me more, isn't it?" Mr. Obama's answer: "I think when you spread the wealth around, it's good for everybody."[1]

The political attacks of the past two years on Wall Street, on greedy bankers, and on capitalism generally are crucial to this claim. The leaders of the 30 percent coalition have articulated a powerful moral argument for their policies, which they elevate far above those of their opponents and their pursuit of "the usual brass rings." The 30 percent coalition say they are working for a better life for ordinary people by standing up to rich people, taking money away from them, and spreading it around.

The 70 percent majority disagrees with this argument, but has done a poor job countering it. Too often, when we debate economic policy, we sound unabashedly materialistic. We talk about growth rates, inflation, and investment while the 30 percent coalition walks off with the claims to happiness and fairness. Rarely do we use the aspirational themes necessary to make the moral case for free people and free markets that we know in our hearts are right.

But the irony is that it is the 30 percent coalition—not the 70 percent majority—that is fundamentally materialistic. They have just been skillful at covering it up. Even as they trot out their latest scheme to expropriate the hard-earned resources of American citizens—from increasingly progressive taxes on income in life to punitive estate taxes at death—the 30 percent coalition charges the majority with money-grubbing selfishness. The truth is precisely the opposite.

The 30 percent coalition possesses a cold, mechanistic view of the world—one that most Americans do not share. What do they believe to be the greatest problem of poor people in America? Insufficient income. What would be evidence of a fairer society? Greater income equality. For the leaders of the 30 percent coalition, money buys happiness, as long as it is distributed fairly. That is why redistribution of income is a fundamental goal, and why free enterprise, which always seems to reward some people and penalize others, cannot be trusted to get things right.

By contrast, the 70 percent majority are New Age radicals. They have simple faith that ingenuity and hard work can and should be rewarded. They admire creative entrepreneurs who have no legal authority and disdain the rule-making bureaucrats who wield pure power. They know that no amount of unearned money can ever heal the human heart: Money is fine, but it is something else entirely—something less tangible and more transcendental—that really brings satisfaction. The 70 percent majority understands that the secret to human flourishing is not money but *earned success* in life.

People flourish when they earn their own success. It's not the money per se, which is merely a measure—not a source—of this earned success. More than any other system, free enterprise enables people to earn success and thereby achieve happiness. For that reason, it is not just an economic alternative but a *moral imperative*. It's not just the most efficient system; it's the most fair and the most just. The 70 percent majority must be able to understand this truth and to defend it. Because if we can't or won't make such a case for free enterprise, the 30 percent coalition will continue to claim the moral high ground, capture a new generation of Americans, and change our culture forever.

The 30 percent coalition in America have long spoken about "economic justice"—the immorality of economic inequality. This is not an original idea. It has been the central organizing element of leftist philosophy for a century and a half. According to Karl Marx, inequality would lead the working classes to revolt, and the final stage of human historical development would come when there were no more social classes and no economic inequalities.

Redistributionists are correct when they point out that economic inequality is on the rise. The U.S. Census Bureau measures economic inequality through what is known as a Gini coefficient, which ranges from zero to one. Zero means no inequality (everyone has the same income), and 1 indicates perfect inequality (a single person has all the income). Between 1970 and 2008, the Gini coefficient in America increased by nearly a fifth, from 0.394 to 0.466.[2]

Income inequality is the issue that most animates the international left wing and the leaders of America's 30 percent coalition. For members of this group, economic inequality is an indicator of unfairness. They do not believe that socioeconomic inequality stems primarily from inequalities of merit or effort. Rather, it comes from discrimination, exploitation, and other sorts of systemic unfairness. And because they believe income inequality makes people unhappy (miserable, actually) through no fault of their own, it is a force of injustice in the world.

In fact, many people—not just the 30 percent coalition—assume that inequality causes unhappiness. It sounds logical and appears to be borne out by the data: Poorer people in almost every community tend to be unhappier than richer people. For example, the 2004 General Social Survey (GSS) found that if you have an annual salary of less than $25,000, you are less than half as likely as someone earning more than $75,000 to describe yourself as "very happy."[3]

It doesn't even matter if you have plenty to get by in life. The data appear to show that simply having less than others makes you unhappy. This proposition was demonstrated in a famous experiment at Harvard University's School of Public Health in 1995, in which a group of students and faculty were asked to choose between earning $50,000 per year while everyone else earned $25,000 or earning $100,000 per year while others made $200,000. The researchers stipulated that prices of goods and services would be the same in both cases, so a higher salary really meant being able to own a nicer home, buy a nicer car, or do whatever else they wanted with the extra money. The results show that those materialistic perquisites matter little to most people: 50 percent chose the first option, hypothetically forgoing $50,000 per year simply to maintain a position of relative affluence.[4]

The 30 percent coalition has always taken these results at face value: Inequality brings misery. Furthermore, they assert, inequality is unjust. They do not believe that merit, hard work, and excellence explain inequality in large part. Rather, they talk first and foremost about prejudice, luck, and advantage-taking as the explanations for why some have so much more than others. The 2005 Maxwell Poll on Civic Engagement and Inequality asked if people agreed with the following statement: "While people may begin with different opportunities [in America], hard work and perseverance can usually overcome those disadvantages." Eight in ten Americans agree, as do more than nine in ten political conservatives. Among those who *disagree*, however, we find more than a third are political liberals with above-average incomes—that is, we find the core of the 30 percent coalition.[5]

A world defined by economic equality, their argument then goes, will be both a fairer and a happier one. And for statists in America, bringing the top down is as good as bringing the bottom up because greater equality is the goal, and it doesn't matter all that much how you get there. One influential liberal economist explains it like this: "If we make taxes commensurate to the damage that an individual does to others when he earns more, then he will only work harder if there is a true net benefit to society as a whole. It is efficient to discourage work effort that makes society worse off." In plain English, tax successful people punitively so they'll work and earn less. This may seem a particularly radical statement, but it is not far from the logical terminus of more mainstream redistributionist arguments.[6]

For the 30 percent coalition, forced redistribution through taxation has other benefits as well. It gets people out of the rat race for things they don't need. They use fewer of the earth's resources and don't lord silly possessions over their neighbors. And with the taxes people pay, the government has more money to do all the things governments do.

Income equality is what the 30 percent coalition wants for America. This is how statists understand the path to greater enlightenment and happiness for the rest of us. And that is why they are so willing to sacrifice entrepreneurship for higher taxes, self-government for growing bureaucracies, individual achievement for powerful unions, and private businesses for federally managed corporations.

The problem with the 30 percent coalition's approach is that it's based on a misreading of statistics and a misunderstanding of the human heart. A careful analysis of the data demonstrates a crucially important truth, and one we overlook to our great peril: *Inequality is not what makes people unhappy.*

To understand this, we need to dig deeper into the concept of earned success. *Earned success* means the ability to create value honestly—not by winning the lottery, not by inheriting a fortune, not by picking up a welfare check. It doesn't even mean making money itself. Earned success is the creation of value in our lives or in the lives of others. Earned success is the stuff of entrepreneurs who seek explosive value through innovation, hard work, and passion. But it isn't just related to commerce. Earned success is also what parents experience when their children do wonderful things, what social innovators feel when they change lives, and what artists feel when they create something of beauty.

People who believe they have earned success—measured in whatever life currency they want—are happy. They are much happier than people who don't believe they've earned their success.

Take the case of work, where typically about half of Americans believe themselves to be successful. In 1996 the General Social Survey asked 500 Americans the following question: "How successful do you feel in your work life?" Some 45 percent of American adults answered "completely successful" or "very successful." The rest said that they were "somewhat successful" or less so. Among the first group, 39 percent said they were very happy in their lives. In the second group, just 20 percent said they were very happy.[7]

This difference in happiness levels is not explained at all by differences in income. Imagine two people who are the same in income, as well as in education, age, sex, race, religion, politics, and family status. But one feels very successful and the other does not. The successful person will be about twice as likely as the other to report feeling "very happy" about his or her life.[8]

But don't forget the "earned" part of success. A 2001 study asked people whether they agreed or disagreed with the statement that they were responsible for their own success. Those who "agreed" or "strongly agreed" with the statement spent 25 percent less time feeling sad than those who "disagreed" or "disagreed strongly" that they were responsible for their own success.[9]

Now, the self-described completely successful or very successful person may well also be richer than the somewhat successful person. That's because money often follows success, particularly when it's success at work. But it's not the money that brings the feeling of success (and hence happiness). The money is just one metric of the value that a person is creating. The data say you can pay one person twice as much as another—it doesn't matter, as long as they both feel successful about their contribution at work. Furthermore, people who earn success in noneconomic pursuits—from fatherhood to voluntarism—can feel the same bliss as the billionaire entrepreneur.

All of this explains why wealthy entrepreneurs continue to work so hard. They already have enough money to meet every need they could ever have, but they still crave earned success like the rest of us, so they are driven to create value at greater and greater heights. The money is just a symbol, important not for what it can buy but for what it says about how some people are contributing and what kind of a difference we are making. The economist Joseph Schumpeter, often called the godfather of modern entrepreneurship, said of entrepreneurs: "The financial result is a secondary consideration, or, at all events, mainly valued as an index of success and as a symptom of victory."[10]

In a country like the United States where people are above the level of subsistence, a poor man who believes he has successfully created something of value will be much better off than a rich man who has not earned his success. The big problem is not that unhappy people have less money than others. It is that they have less earned success.[11]

Your mother was right: Money can't buy happiness. Many people give lip service to this idea, but many still mistake the symbol of success for success itself and chase after money as if it were the elixir of pure joy. People—even rich people—do lots of crazy things for money: They lie, they steal, and they cheat. They spend more and more hours at work and neglect their families. They fight their siblings over the terms of their inheritance.

Money is the first thing a lot of people turn to when they think about what's missing in their lives. When you ask people what would make them immediately happier than they are at present, they frequently talk about money. A pay raise, winning the lottery, a surprise inheritance, a check from the government, or some other unexpected financial windfall—these are the kinds of things people often believe will bring them a happier life. And this doesn't just apply to the destitute or to those who have lost their jobs, but to the rest of us, too.

But what do the data tell us? They tell us that on a national level, pumping more money into an already wealthy economy does not in itself make citizens happier. America has gotten much richer during the past several decades, but happiness levels have not risen accordingly. In 1972, for example, 30 percent of Americans said they were very happy, and the average American enjoyed about $25,000 (in today's dollars) of our nation's total income. By 2004, the percentage of very happy Americans stayed virtually unchanged, at 31 percent, while the share of national income had skyrocketed to $38,000 (a 50 percent increase in average income).[12]

Our dramatic increase in wealth has done little for our national happiness—and studies indicate that the same holds true in other countries. There is only one exception to this rule: Nations in abject poverty do become happier, on average, when suffering is alleviated through increased wealth and income. But for countries above the level of survival, raising the average income won't raise the life satisfaction of the citizenry.[13]

Maybe you're thinking that this is all very interesting but not particularly relevant to your own life. Perhaps the whole country wouldn't get happier if average incomes rose. But if you suddenly got richer, you'd be much happier, right? No, you wouldn't—not unless you truly earned it, and then it would be because of the success, not the money.

The truth is that if you were simply given a pot of unearned cash, it wouldn't improve your life. One of the best known studies showing this examines lottery winners. This type of gaming tends to be played by folks without a lot of money to begin with, so it provides useful insight into the effects of sudden unearned wealth. In 1978, researchers at the University of Michigan tracked down and interviewed a group of major lottery winners. They found that although the newly rich experienced an immediate boost to their cheeriness, their mood darkened within months to levels around where they were to begin with.[14]

But there's worse news. The initial high that came from winning actually reduced the impact of simple pleasures—things like talking with a friend, getting a compliment, or buying clothes. Further, the lottery win diminished the happiness derived from all the new pleasures made possible by the sudden increase in wealth. That is, these people found little happiness in buying a new car or house. In short, the glow from getting rich wears off quickly. Old pleasures in life become less enjoyable, and spending the money just isn't that great.

The same results emerge in studies of other kinds of unearned income. Take welfare payments, for example. When a person loses her job, she may well seek public assistance until landing new employment. Although this may make sense from a public policy point of view, it does not help her happiness. According to the University of Michigan's 2001 Panel Study of Income Dynamics, going on the welfare rolls increases by 16 percent the likelihood of a person saying she has felt inconsolably sad over the past month. Correlation is not causation, to be sure, and the misery of welfare recipients probably goes well beyond the welfare check itself. Nonetheless, studies show that welfare recipients are far unhappier than equally poor people who do not get welfare checks.[15]

Money doesn't buy happiness because money per se isn't bringing any earned success. When a person's income spikes, he immediately reacts to the changed circumstances, usually with corresponding spikes in his sense of what "a lot of money" is. The increased income, in effect, merely "resets the bar." Economists describe this process of adaptation as the "hedonic treadmill." A sudden increase in income merely speeds up the pace of the treadmill, but unless we are succeeding in something besides accumulating money, we never actually make any forward movement toward happiness. (How depressing.)

People think that they will be happier if they have more money, but they quickly find out that they're mistaken. When people are asked what income they require for a satisfying life, they consistently respond—regardless of their income—that they would need an income about 40 percent higher than whatever they're earning at the time. For instance, a $50,000 earner may say that his required income is around $70,000. But if that person gets a $20,000 raise, his estimation of his required income will also rise—and he'll soon be bugging his employer for something closer to a six-figure salary.[16]

Founding Father Benjamin Franklin (a pretty rich man for his time) grasped the truth about money's inability to deliver life satisfaction. "Money never made a man happy yet, nor will it," he declared. "The more a man has, the more he wants. Instead of filling a vacuum, it makes one."

If money without earned success does not bring happiness, then redistributing money won't make for a happier America. Knowing as we do that earning success is the key to happiness, rather than simply getting more money, the goal of our political system should be this: to give all Americans the greatest opportunities possible to succeed based on their hard work and merit. And that's exactly what the free-enterprise system does— makes earned success possible for the most people. This is the *liberty* our founders wrote about, the liberty that enables the true *pursuit of happiness*.

The 30 percent coalition's pursuit of redistribution and income equality will never deliver on their promises for better lives.

There are three reasons why earned success delivers happiness: optimism, meaning, and control over our lives.

Optimism

If we know we have the possibility of earning success, we know we can improve our lives and our lot. That is one of the great gifts of the American free-enterprise system—the opportunity for people to reinvent themselves, to work toward a future that is better than their past. This is the American Dream. For immigrants from around the world, the United States represents the land of second chances, a place where you have the possibility of determining what you will become.

People who are optimistic about their chances to succeed tend to be much happier than those who are pessimistic. Optimists may be rich or poor, educated or uneducated, but they all believe that they can better themselves in life and get ahead through perseverance and hard work (they can earn their success), and this gives them happiness. In 2004, the General Social Survey presented a sample of Americans with the following statement and asked whether they agreed or disagreed: "The way things are in America, people like me and my family have a good chance of improving our standard of living." Those who agree are 44 percent more likely than those who disagree to say they are very happy in life. The optimists are also 40 percent less likely than the pessimists to say they feel like they are "no good at all" at times, and they are 20 percent less likely to say they feel like a failure.[17]

In America there is a distinct "optimism gap" between left and right. Conservatives are by and large more optimistic than liberals. Even poor conservatives are more optimistic than rich liberals. Take the 2005 Maxwell Poll on Civic Engagement and Inequality, which asked, "How much upward mobility—children doing better than the family they come from—do you think there is in America: a lot, some, or not much?" Although 48 percent of below-average income conservatives say "a lot," only 26 percent of upper-income liberals give this answer. Meanwhile, 90 percent of poorer conservatives agreed with the following proposition: "While people may begin with different opportunities, hard work and perseverance can usually overcome those disadvantages." Just 65 percent of richer liberals agree. The liberal-conservative differences on these questions persist even if we control not just for income, but also for education, sex, family situation, religion, and race.[18]

It is therefore no surprise that conservatives are much happier than liberals in America. According to the 2004 General Social Survey, 44 percent of respondents who call themselves "conservative" or "very conservative" say they are "very happy." This compares with just 25 percent of people who call themselves "liberal" or "very liberal." Adults on the political right are only half as likely as those on the left to say, "At times, I think I am no good at all." They are also less likely to say they are dissatisfied with themselves, that they are inclined to feel like a failure, or that they are pessimistic about their futures. This "happiness gap" between conservatives and liberals has persisted for at least 30 years. It does not matter which party is in political power.[19]

Regardless of political opinions, for optimism to persist in America, people have to continue to be able to get ahead. They need to know that their efforts will be rewarded and that hard work will result in measurable achievement. Only in such circumstances will they happily strive. We know money is not the same thing as earned success. And we might like people to keep their eyes on the value they create and not the size of their paychecks. But we also know that money is easy to measure, and not surprisingly, it affects behavior when the government takes it away from people. For example, a great deal of economic research shows that progressive taxation lowers work effort—and has even been found to drive up illegal activity.[20]

Progressive taxation dismantles the cause-and-effect relationship between working hard and achieving success. Everyone knows we need taxes to pay for key services. But taxes for the simple purpose of income redistribution—a staple of the 30 percent coalition—is all pain, no gain, when it comes to optimism.

Increasing the progressivity of income taxes—a policy that has been central to the 30 percent's plans—is also just bad fiscal policy. Generation after generation, the evidence shows that increasing taxes on the wealthy raises virtually no revenues. In the view of many economists tax revenues will actually decline in the long run because of the negative impact on the incentives for successful people to work and earn.[21]

Even worse than highly progressive personal income taxes is taxing business. For the 30 percent coalition, however, there is nothing fairer, especially when it comes to "big business." The nameless, faceless plutocrats running Fortune 500 firms are an easy target, despite the fact that America already has some of the highest corporate taxes in the world. These government levies on doing business are a job-killer, though, and filter down to kill optimism among ordinary people.

Most Americans have a hard time believing it, but we tax our companies at higher levels than the Europeans tax theirs. In fact, 2009 marks the twelfth year in a row in which U.S. rates have been higher than those in the rest of the Organization for Economic Cooperation and Development (OECD). And while we sock it to American entrepreneurs, our competitors are cutting corporate taxes. In 2009, for example, Canada, Sweden, the Czech Republic, and Korea all reduced their rates. The United States remains second only to Japan for the highest rates in the OECD.[22]

You probably didn't know that America is a high-tax country, compared to, say, Sweden. That's because you've been told over and over again that in America we give rich people and businesses a pass.

But remind yourself of the facts every time you hear about American jobs going overseas. Remember, too, that other governments are competing with America to provide a tax-friendly home for entrepreneurs—and a source of jobs and optimism for their citizens. Then ask your congressional representative why punishing companies that remain in America is fairer than nourishing the free enterprise that is the lifeblood for our economy, creating jobs and growth for Americans.

As in the case of income taxes, corporate taxes don't even bring in as much revenue as they would if they were lower. Economists Kevin Hassett and Alex Brill calculated the corporate tax rate that would produce the most revenue. Their result: 26 percent. Reducing the corporate rate from the current 39 percent, they found, would actually increase tax revenues as a share of gross domestic product (GDP). The benefits of reducing corporate taxes don't stop there. By cutting such rates, the United States would also be encouraging foreign firms to locate here, offering more opportunity to our citizens—as well as increasing tax revenues.[23]

But there is one simple reason why politicians avoid reducing corporate taxes. Because it looks like a gift to the rich—to company owners and wealthy stockholders. Never mind that small businesses would benefit from such a tax cut, just like large corporations, that rich people pay taxes on their income, and that fully 47 percent of U.S. households own stocks or bonds. Corporations are easy to pick on; that's all. Everything comes down to the 30 percent coalition's understanding of "fairness," which is really just income equality.[24]

The great irony here is that President Obama is probably the only politician who could successfully lower corporate taxes. No Republican would dare try it for fear of the liberal demagoguery that would surely follow. But President Obama would first have to loosen the grip that the 30 percent coalition has over his economic policies and improve his comprehension of the source of optimism—opportunity—that Americans need to earn their success.

Meaning

Earned success gives people a sense of meaning about their lives. And meaning also is a key to human flourishing. It reassures us that what we do in life is of significance and value, for ourselves and those around us. To truly flourish, we need to know that the ways in which we occupy our waking hours are not based on the mere pursuit of pleasure or money or any other superficial goal. We need to know that our endeavors have a deeper purpose.

Meaning in life is derived from lots of things; Religion and family spring most readily to mind. These institutions allow people to say that they live for something beyond themselves and beyond the here and now. A huge amount of research shows that married people and religious people are much happier than singles and secularists.[25]

Work is another tremendously important source of meaning for Americans. When asked by the General Social Survey to rate on a scale of 1–7 the importance of deriving meaning from a job, 84 percent give it a 6 or a 7.[26]

It doesn't seem to matter if the work is unpleasant or even dangerous, as long as it is meaningful. In fact, if it entails sacrifice for a cause greater than ourselves, levels of meaning may be even greater. As Viennese psychiatrist and Holocaust survivor Victor Frankl learned, meaning can be found in work in the most desperate of circumstances. In his (aptly titled) memoir, *Man's Search for Meaning*, Frankl describes how he and others derived a sense of meaning as laborers in a German concentration camp during World War II.[27]

Free enterprise enables us to find meaningful work through free markets that match our skills and passions. In free markets, we can change jobs, work longer or shorter hours within reason, and take more or less vacation than other people. Increasingly, we can flex our hours and jump into and out of the workforce as our lives and our circumstances change. These free markets largely do not exist in Europe, with their mandated pay and vacation, cradle-to-grave systems of job security, and generous unemployment benefits. The 30 percent coalition looks at Europe and sees a better life precisely because labor markets are not free and workers there enjoy more security.

So who is happier at work—America or Europe? The 2002 International Social Survey Programme showed that Americans are 46 percent likelier than the French to say they are "completely satisfied" with their jobs. Similarly, Americans are 52 percent likelier than Germans, 42 percent likelier than the British, and about 190 percent likelier than the Spanish to experience complete job satisfaction.[28]

People are surprisingly satisfied with their jobs in America. And despite the populist stories of blue-collar discontent, satisfaction is not limited to white-collar workers. According to the 2002 GSS, 89 percent of working Americans say they are very satisfied or somewhat satisfied with their jobs. Precisely the same share of those with incomes above and below the average are satisfied: 89 percent. Similarly, 88 percent of people without a college education are satisfied, as well as 87 percent of people who refer to themselves as "working class."[29]

Americans like their work so much, in fact, that most would continue doing it even if they didn't have to. In 2002 the GSS asked, "If you were to get enough money to live as comfortably as you would like for the rest of your life, would you continue to work or would you stop working?" Only 31 percent of American adults say they would stop working. Sixty-nine percent of American adults say that they would continue working even if they did not need to. Again, these numbers cut across socioeconomic lines. There is no difference at all between those with below- and above-average incomes. Similarly, 66 percent of people without a college education would keep working.

Meaning at work comes from feeling productive. This is how we earn our success and what makes us happy. People who feel they are productive in their jobs, regardless of pay, are about five times likelier to be very satisfied with their jobs than people who don't feel this way. Of course, when we are being productive, we often get paid more. But the money is a nice side effect, and not the cause of the happiness we enjoy.[30]

Feeling productive does not mean being protected from competition. It means beating the competition through merit and hard work. It does not come from a collective bargaining agreement and the threat to strike, but from a job well done. And it certainly doesn't come from a welfare check. All of this explains why our free-enterprise system produces happier workers than in most of Europe.

We can learn from Europe about corporate taxes but not about labor policy. Because of rigid labor laws across the European Union, it is hard to lay off workers or even fire them for just cause. Employers are therefore more hesitant to hire workers in the first place, which has resulted in significant unemployment, especially among the young. In France about a quarter of young adults are jobless; in Spain more than 40 percent.[31]

While this has happiness-diminishing consequences for the unemployed, it also has a negative effect on those who do have jobs. If you know that finding a new position will be difficult or impossible, you will hold on to the job you have, even if it is a bad match for your interests or skills. And in such a situation, you can probably say goodbye to any notion of deriving meaning through work. Instead, European workers increasingly seek meaning in activities outside of work—and now have the shortened workweeks, extended vacations, and early retirement programs that make this possible.

Americans prefer to find meaning in their jobs rather than through their after-work pursuits and to trade security of employment for the possibilities of earned success. The free-enterprise system reflects these American priorities. The policies of the 30 percent coalition (strengthened labor unions, 20-year-and-out public sector jobs, and other statist, European-style interventions) do not.

Control

The ability to exercise control in our daily lives is the other effect of earned success. Successful, flourishing—happy—people are those who believe that through their own efforts they can determine their own destinies. Those who are powerless, and unable to affect what they consider important aspects of their lives, are among the most miserable people of all.

We all want control over our lives. Free enterprise gives us this control; statism takes it away. Whereas free enterprise respects the role of the individual in pursuing his own interests, the state prefers to exercise control on its citizens' behalf, thereby diminishing for them an important avenue to personal fulfillment and happiness.

Entrepreneurs will tell you that one of the greatest satisfactions in life is "being your own boss." Gallup finds that business owners have the highest overall well-being and job satisfaction of any occupational group in America. This is despite the fact that self-employed business owners work longer hours than anyone else and the fact that they earn less money on average than professionals and executives who work for companies owned by other people. By contrast, low-control, union jobs in manufacturing score worst in well-being. One study from 1979 not only found that unionized workers experienced lower levels of job satisfaction, on average, than their nonunionized counterparts. It also found that the job misery for union members got worse over time, with increasing levels of dissatisfaction the longer they stayed in their jobs.[32]

One British study also claims that entrepreneurship is good for one's health. The study finds that in a comparison between entrepreneurs and employees, entrepreneurs scored significantly better. They enjoyed lower blood pressure and lower somatic and mental morbidity, as well as more favorable behavioral indicators, such as number of sick days and physician visits.[33]

I once faced a professional riddle. At nineteen, I dropped out of college to take a full-time job playing chamber music. I made little money and spent months every year driving around America in a van with four other guys. Once we drove straight from Baltimore to San Francisco, stopping only for gas. But it was a great job. I had control over my artistic destiny, liked my colleagues, and every night played music that I helped choose. After six years, I quit that job to play with a symphony orchestra in Spain. I expected to love it—great music, really good money, a fun place to live, and no van trips. But I was miserable. Why the difference?

The answer was control. The more control you have over your life, the more responsible you feel for your own success (or failure). And as we've seen, the more you feel you've earned your success, the happier your life will be. I had a lot of control (and a lot of happiness) playing chamber music. In the orchestra, I was under the thumb of a conductor and had no say in my repertoire or schedule. And my experience, it turns out, is representative. A 1994 Harvard study of various types of workers found that orchestra musicians have moderately low job satisfaction.[34]

Emerging research shows that control is a powerful secret to success in business. In a recent book, authors Brian Carney and Isaac Getz reveal that the most prosperous companies across a broad spectrum of industries are the ones that give their employees the freedom to take risks and follow their own ideas.[35]

But it's not just control at work that matters. We thrive when we have control across all areas of our lives, even those that might seem insignificant. In 1976 psychologists in Connecticut decided to investigate the effects of control on senior citizens' well-being. They selected a nursing home and applied a simple experiment in the way the residents were treated on two different floors. On one floor residents were given control over their movie night, and they were allowed to choose and care for the plants on their floor. On the other floor residents were not given the same choices and responsibilities. These tiny differences had huge effects. The first group of seniors—no healthier or happier than the second when the experiment began—quickly showed greater alertness, more activity, and better mood. A year and a half later they were still doing better and, remarkably, were even dying at only half the rate of the residents on the second floor.[36]

What is true in orchestras and nursing homes is also true in political and economic systems. Where citizens have more control in their economies, you find happier populations. We can calculate this by comparing the happiness of citizens with their economic freedom, as economists typically measure it. The *Wall Street Journal* and Heritage Foundation's annual *Index of Economic Freedom* ranks dozens of nations on a scale of 1 to 100 with respect to ten freedoms: business freedom, trade freedom, fiscal freedom, government spending, monetary freedom, investment freedom, financial freedom, property rights, freedom from corruption, and labor freedom.[37]

Matching economic freedom data with happiness indexes, we clearly find that freer people are happier people. A one-point increase in economic freedom is associated with a two-point rise in the percentage of the population saying they are completely happy or very happy. Yet these facts elude the statists—those who would take our control and hand it over to the government for the public good.[38]

All governments need to exercise some control, of course. Indeed, the whole world of public policy can probably be reduced to the question of how much. At the moment, the American people are thinking long and hard about that question because many of our leaders are strongly of the view that the current level of government control is insufficient.

Governments always think this, though. Politicians believe they were elected to do things, not to not do things, and this generally means grabbing control away from citizens. In nation after nation, government has been steadily growing in power and size. Right here in America, from 2005 to 2009 alone, government spending as a percentage of GDP grew from 35 percent to 43 percent. Nearly half of every dollar we create in this country today is dedicated to the ever-growing state. How much is too much? The 30 percent coalition thinks we're not there yet. They think we need to tax more, spend more, and spread more money around.[39]

One clear example of the 30 percent coalition's disregard for control was its push for "Obamacare"—the Democratic reform of the U.S. health system, over the clear objections of a majority of the American people (polls showed support for Obamacare below 40 percent as of September 2009).[40]

The health care legislation represents a massive government intrusion into the lives of Americans. It will raise the cost of care for some Americans and lower it (even to zero) for others. According to most economists, under Obamacare average Americans will have to pay more for, at best, the health care they currently enjoy. Their increased health dollars will be

redistributed through taxes and subsidies to those who are currently uninsured or, in the view of government officials,
insufficiently insured.[41]

Obamacare will make Americans less happy because it will
diminish their sense of control by taking health choices away
from citizens and handing them over to bureaucrats. The plan
effectively limits choice across the entire spectrum of health
care. what kind of health insurance citizens can buy, what kind
of doctors they can see, what kind of procedures their doctors
will perform, what kind of drugs they can take, and what treatment options they may have.[42]

Meanwhile, Obamacare will limit the ability of people to
choose affordable insurance coverage through less comprehensive, consumer-driven insurance plans. Incredibly, the
White House even opposed the small degree of control that will
come from letting Americans shop for health care plans from
out-of-state insurance companies.

But reducing control isn't the only way Obamacare will
lower happiness. As was the case with mortgage default, the
health plan rewards bad behavior in a way that seems unfair to
Americans. Consider, for example, the promise to provide
health insurance to nearly all, regardless of preexisting conditions. This at first seems appealing. But think about it: If people
don't have to worry about taking out insurance until they need
it, many won't buy it. And this is unfair to the rest of us, who
carry insurance in good times and bad and will subsidize those
who do not. (According to the Census Bureau, 21 percent of
those currently uninsured live in households earning at least

$75,000 a year—reasonably well-off people, many of whom have opted not to purchase health care coverage.)[43]

It's possible that Obamacare might even lead to a *decline* in the number of people with insurance. This is the view of economist Martin Feldstein, who calls it the plan's "nasty surprise." His reasoning goes like this: If you can't be turned down for a preexisting condition, then why not drop your coverage, save the premiums, and take out a policy only if you have a serious illness? Feldstein's research shows that it is cost-effective for people to go uninsured, thereby placing their health costs onto the rest of us. To me—and probably to you—this cannot be understood as "fair."[44]

Obamacare is the 30 percent coalition's agenda writ large. It deprives Americans of control in an important aspect of their lives, and is unfair. And that is why they have repudiated it in public opinion polls, in popular protests, and at the ballot box.

The rival positions in the burgeoning culture war are now clear.

The 30 percent coalition believes in income equality and that any one legal source of income is as good as any other. They believe that it should make no difference whether income comes from redistribution and government edict or from enterprise and excellence as judged by the free market. This is an ideology driven by raw materialism.

In contrast, the 70 percent majority maintains a worldview that is primarily nonmaterialistic. It understands money as just a proxy measure of true prosperity and personal fulfillment. It emphasizes creativity, meaning, optimism, and control in one's own life and seeks to escape from under the heavy hand of the state. It is traditional in its American values yet perpetually new in its outlook. It naturally disdains the soul-sapping nature of Big Bureaucracy and the protected mediocrity of Big Labor, and has a healthy suspicion of the Faustian tendencies of Big Business—divorced from the entrepreneur's ethics—to crawl into bed with the government.

To win the culture war, the 70 percent majority must find a way to reclaim the morality of their worldview. Those of us in the free-enterprise movement must show that while we often use the language of commerce and business, what we really believe in is human flourishing and happiness. We must artic- ulate a set of moral principles that set forth our fundamental values and principles and be prepared to defend them against attack. The following is the first and most important of these moral principles: *The purpose of free enterprise is human flour- ishing, not materialism.* Free enterprise is not simply an economic alternative. Free enterprise is about who we are as a people and who we want to be. It embodies our power as indi- viduals and our independence from the government. In short, enterprise is an act of self-expression—a declaration of what we truly value—and a social issue for Americans.

When we reduce the idea of work to nothing more than a means of economic support, we strip it of its transcendental meaning in our lives. When we talk about business only as an economic engine, we forget that it can and should represent our values and give us a way to improve our world. And when we talk about entrepreneurship as nothing more than a method to attain economic growth, we miss what truly drives entrepreneurs and what (for the time being at least) makes America culturally different from the other nations of the world.

It is hugely ironic that the 30 percent coalition accuses the 70 percent majority of materialism. When we reject their taxes and argue against their government spending, they say we are selfish and care more about money than people. And we are complicit when we fight back only with arguments about efficiency and economic incentives. They talk about the soul while we talk about money—when free enterprise does far more for the human soul than any amount of redistribution ever can.

We need to find a better language with which to talk about our free enterprise values. And that is the subject of the next chapter.

CHAPTER FOUR

The Moral Case for Free Enterprise

T HE BLATANT ATTEMPT to impose 30 percent values on a 70 percent nation has resulted in a predictable phenomenon: backlash from citizens across America.

The first sign of rebellion against the 30 percent coalition came in the spring of 2009 with the Taxed Enough Already (Tea Party) protests. In these grassroots demonstrations, hundreds of thousands of Americans joined together to make public their support for the free-enterprise system—and their opposition to the explosion of government spending, unaccountable bureaucratic power, and the state's willingness to prop up those who had engaged in corporate malfeasance and mortgage fraud.

Most Americans sympathize with the Tea Party protestors. According to a Rasmussen poll conducted less than a week after the initial demonstrations, more than half of Americans viewed the protests favorably, and of these, one-third viewed them "very favorably." Nearly a year later, in February 2010, a FOX

News/Opinion Dynamics poll found that 61 percent of people who know about the Tea Party movement have a positive opinion of it. The poll also showed that among those with an opinion, a bit more than 70 percent agree that the Tea Party movement is "a serious group of people who believe government is too big and taxes are too high and it should be taken seriously." The other 30 percent regard it as "a fringe group of people with extreme right-wing views about government that should not be taken seriously." So which side do the media come down on—the 70 percent majority's, or the 30 percent coalition's? You guessed it: The protestors are portrayed as little more than a radical element—suspicious, ignorant backwoodsmen automatically opposed to virtually anything the politicians in Washington might do.[1]

For the media, the protesters were simply too dim to understand the policy issues at hand. At a rally in Chicago, a CNN reporter asked one man why he was protesting. But just as he began to talk about "the people's right to liberty," she cut him off: "Sir, what does this have to do with your taxes? Do you realize that you're eligible for a $400 credit?"[2]

Another popular flare-up against statism came in the summer of 2009 in response to "Obamacare"—the president's bid to expand greatly the government's role in American health care. Citizens flocked to town hall meetings to confront their legislators about a proposed health care plan that threatened to place their health care choices in the hands of the government. Many politicians tried to dismiss the protests. In this, they were again aided by the press, which largely portrayed the protestors as extremists or agents of the health care industry.

The charges are false: Survey data show that the views of these citizens are far from extreme. A January 2010 poll found that 51 percent of Americans oppose the president's health care plan, with only 39 percent in favor. And an August 2009 poll found that 61 percent of those polled believe that the town hall protesters are mainly individual citizens coming together to express their views. Only 28 percent—the 30 percent coalition, more or less—buys the idea that they were mainly coordinated by health care interest groups.[3]

If the media tried to dismiss the Tea Party and town hall protesters, they were less able to ignore the voters of Massachusetts in January 2010. The earlier protests had been a warning shot in the burgeoning culture war. But with the election of little-known Republican Scott Brown to the deceased senator Ted Kennedy's seat in a special off-cycle election, the American mainstream actually drew blood.

After Senator Kennedy's death in 2009, there seemed little doubt that his Senate seat was safe for Democrats. After all, Kennedy was arguably the most liberal man in the U.S. Senate and had held the seat for an amazing 46 years. Furthermore, his putative successor, Massachusetts Attorney General Martha Coakley, had led the polls by thirty points in the weeks leading up to the election.[4]

But Brown was in touch with America's political mainstream. He won by declaring himself not an apparatchik Republican but an enthusiast for free enterprise. In his words, "What made America great? Free markets, free enterprise, manufacturing, job creation. That's how we're gonna do it, not by enlarging government." His cultural pitch for capitalism hit just the right chord even in the extremely liberal state of Massachusetts. Brown's election was not just a repudiation of the Democrats' unpopular health care bill. It was also a rejection of big government programs, higher taxes, and growing debt. It struck at the heart of the 30 percent coalition's agenda for America.[5]

The 30 percent coalition suffered important setbacks over the course of Barack Obama's presidency. And the left's narrative about the financial crisis—what won them the 2008 election—is beginning to ring hollow to millions. In January 2010, a CNN/Opinion Research poll found that 74 percent of Americans feel that at least half the economic stimulus spending has been wasted. Sixty-three percent believe that the spending had been guided by purely political ends and will have no economic benefit. In his first year in office, public disapproval for President Obama's handling of the economy climbed from 30 percent to 61 percent, according to a Gallup poll.[6]

Still, the 30 percent *kulturkampf* against traditional American values goes on. They have been wounded by the recent backlash and in the months ahead will be seeking to regroup and regain the initiative. For those determined to fight for the preservation of America's free-enterprise culture, the most intense phases of the battle are still ahead.

Victory in that battle is far from sure. To win, the 70 percent majority will need to come together right now around a coherent set of core principles. It is not enough simply to oppose the ideas of the 30 percent coalition. We need clear, positive principles that lead to better ideas. These are not just about differences over how to organize an economy and maximize the production of goods and services. They are matters of a higher level—about the moral superiority of the free-enterprise system over the forces of statism and redistribution. These principles should remind us what really matters and keep us from getting stuck in the old arguments over money. They are principles that should rally the 70 percent majority in the battle for the soul of America. In the last chapter, I introduced the first of these principles, which is at the very center of the free-enterprise movement:

- The purpose of free enterprise is human flourishing, not materialism.

This chapter adds four more principles to complement the first.

- We stand for equality of opportunity, not equality of income.
- We seek to stimulate true prosperity, not treat poverty.
- America can and should be a gift to the world.
- What truly matters is principle, not political power.

Together, these principles can serve as a guide to the policies that will win the future.

America Stands for Equality of Opportunity, Not Equality of Income

As many non-Americans will tell you, Americans are the most egalitarian people in the world. If you don't believe it, ask yourself (assuming you are American) whether you think it is all right for a legal immigrant to work hard in America and succeed just like anybody else. Chances are, you wouldn't just accept this idea—you would actually fight for it. That's uniquely American. In other countries, nothing irritates the natives more than a rich immigrant.

Yes, in America we stand for equality. But for the large majority of us, this means equality of opportunity, not equality of outcome. If you are like most Americans, you believe we all should start at more or less the same place, with more or less the same opportunities to succeed in life. But you also believe that, within reason, it's perfectly all right if we end up in different places. Whether or not we succeed should depend on our abilities and our efforts. This principle lies at the heart of what it means to be an American and dates back to our national founding. As James Madison put it, the "first object of government is the protection of different and unequal faculties of acquiring property."[7]

If you are in the 70 percent majority, you believe that everyone should get a chance to succeed. Or they should fail on their own merits. If this leads to income inequality—above some acceptable floor—so be it.

The intellectual and political leaders of the 30 percent coalition deeply disagree. They prefer a world in which we all end up in roughly the same economic place regardless of our abilities and efforts.

This fundamental difference in worldview leads to a major disagreement about the role of government. The majority believes government should protect the returns for hard work and merit. The 30 percent coalition effectively wants the government to penalize success. In 2009, 63 percent of Americans agreed that "government policies should promote opportunity by fostering job growth, encouraging entrepreneurs, and allowing people to keep more of what they earn." But 31 percent disagreed, favoring instead, "Government policies should promote fairness by narrowing the gap between rich and poor, spreading the wealth, and making sure that economic outcomes are more equal." This is America's culture war in a nutshell.[8]

Abraham Lincoln put the 70 percent majority's opinion most succinctly when he declared, "I don't believe in a law to prevent a man from getting rich; it would do more harm than good. So while we do not propose any war upon capital, we do wish to allow the humblest man an equal chance to get rich with everybody else."[9]

The redistributionist principles espoused by the 30 percent coalition lie in stark contrast to majority American values. The 30 percent coalition knows this full well, so they don't come right out and say what they believe. You never hear them say, "Rich people should be brought down, no matter how industrious they are. And poor people should be brought up, no matter how bad their personal choices." Instead, the 30 percent coalition has found a lofty-sounding euphemism to justify income redistribution. The word it most often uses is *fairness*.

In 2008, presidential candidate Barack Obama promised to raise taxes on individuals earning more than $200,000 a year and on couples earning more than $250,000. His rationale was this: We needed "a sense of balance and fairness in our tax code." Over and over again, he has asserted the need for well-off Americans to "pay their fair share."[10]

Judge for yourself whether our tax system is unfair in favor of the rich. In America, the top 5 percent of earners bring in 37 percent of the income but pay 60 percent of the federal income taxes. The bottom 50 percent earn 12 percent of the income but pay 3 percent of the taxes.[11]

We often hear that America is less progressive in its taxation than the social democracies in Europe. That is increasingly a false claim. From 1986 to 2006 the proportion of taxes that the top 1 percent of income earners paid grew from 26 percent to 40 percent. With President Obama's original tax plan, nearly half of all tax filers in America would have paid nothing in federal income taxes in 2011.[12]

The idea that the rich do not pay their fair share in this system simply does not stand up to any normal understanding of fairness. What redistributionists mean by "fair" is a tax payment that simply equalizes incomes more than they are at present. At some point, the "rich" (as defined by the 30 percent) will pay *all* the income taxes in America. For the 30 percent coalition, this is fair and just. For the 70 percent majority, this is unfair and unjust. Remember, two-thirds of Americans believe that *everybody* should have to pay something.[13]

The 30 percent coalition's definition of fairness, fundamentally at odds with the worldview of the 70 percent majority, is a huge potential liability for them. They have concealed the central pillar of their ideology—income equality—under a misleading definition of fairness. They say one thing but mean another. The 70 percent majority needs to expose this fact and reclaim the language of fairness for the free-enterprise system.

The 30 percent coalition is clever when it comes to redistribution. They would have you believe that income equality is equivalent to equality in other areas, such as law or politics or religion. And because America, the world's first modern democracy, was founded on the principle of equality, their rhetoric can seem highly compelling if you don't think too deeply about it.

Americans believe in equality before a court of law and consider it a moral issue. It doesn't matter "how guilty you look." Everyone is supposed to get due process; all are equally presumed innocent until proven guilty through a trial. And even more morally outrageous is the thought that our justice system would treat people differently based on their ethnicity or race. When it comes to the law, Lady Justice is blindfolded. If this is not the case, as in the pre–Civil Rights South for African Americans, we are outraged. Our natural sense of justice demands a change in policy.

We also believe in political equality: "one man, one vote." In America the beggar enters the polling booth on the same terms as the billionaire. We would not tolerate it any other way. This is what makes us different from—and morally superior to—many other countries.

Americans, especially those with strong Judeo-Christian principles, also believe in the equality of individuals before God. According to some passages in the New Testament, the poor may even be at an advantage. This is not just consolation for the poor. It is a principle of transcendent justice.[14]

Legal equality, political equality, religious equality—almost all Americans would agree that these values are vital to our nation. But equality of income? That's a fundamentally different kind of equality. We can all agree that everyone has an equal right to a fair trial, but we certainly don't all agree that everyone has a right to receive a verdict of "innocent." Only the innocent people deserve that! Likewise with our political system, we believe that everyone has the right to vote, but we don't believe that everyone has the right to see their chosen candidate elected to office.

This is what makes the 30 percent coalition's reliance on the rhetoric of fairness so duplicitous. It implies that equality of outcome is a core American principle, when in fact what Americans believe in is equality of opportunity and the potential to earn success. That is why, for example, we have a strong commitment to universal education in this country. While we may be troubled by teachers' unions and grinding education bureaucracies, we still favor the funding of public schools. Everybody should have the same chance to succeed through learning.

The 30 percent coalition twists equality of opportunity into equality of outcome. They elevate money to the level of justice by saying that this must be more equal too. Whether conscious or not, calls for redistribution for the sake of equalizing incomes serve the same goals as Karl Marx's famous formula of "From each according to his ability, to each according to his need."

For the sake of their notion of fairness, leaders of the 30 percent coalition are almost as happy to bring the top down as they are to push the bottom up. Occasionally, some of them will admit it. One prominent American political philosopher has influentially advocated "market constitutionalism," which would, like constitutional democracy, "set similar limits on the economic power of the wealthiest men and women." He advocated this simply because he was offended—and believes we should be too—by the idea of people having too much money.[15]

How do we fight against the redistributive tendencies of the 30 percent coalition? You can point out that redistribution is inconsistent with mainstream views. You can point out that equality of income is wildly materialistic or that taxing the rich more and more will lower overall economic opportunity for everybody—especially the poor. You can make these logical points until you're blue in the face. But for the leaders of the 30 percent coalition, arguing against income redistribution is like arguing against equality before the law. For them, it's a moral issue, pure and simple.

Admittedly, it is easy to be intimidated by the rhetoric of "fairness." Nobody wants to sound antipoor. It is no surprise, therefore, that many in the 70 percent majority have chosen just to cede to the 30 percent coalition the fairness issue and content ourselves with making the case for economic efficiency. "Sure, socialism may be fairer to the poor," you may have found yourself saying, "but it's terrible for the economy."

Proponents of free enterprise must not make this mistake. Fairness should not be a 30 percent trump card but rather its Achilles' heel. Equality of income is not fair. It is distinctly *un*fair. If you work harder than a coworker but are paid the same, that is unfair. If you save your money but still retire with the same pension as your spendthrift neighbor, that is unfair. And if you stay in your house and make the mortgage payments even when its value drops but your neighbor walks away from his without recourse, that is unfair.

Fairness is a system that rewards hard work, merit, and excellence. It is a system that rewards the honest makers in society. We do not have to punish the takers, but we certainly should not punish the makers. Real fairness does not mean bringing the top down (beyond procuring the funding we actually need for a functioning state). It means giving the bottom a fighting chance to rise.

Yes, this system will produce unequal outcomes. We should not be ashamed of that. As long as everyone has the same opportunities, the free-enterprise movement should have no qualms about trumpeting our values as deeply American and profoundly fair.

We are committed to the belief that fairness lies in equality of opportunity rather than equality of outcome. Still, we all are deeply troubled by poverty both around the world and in America.

The 30 percent coalition has done a skillful job painting us as callous when it comes to the poor. Opponents of income redistribution, they argue, just don't care about the plight of the less fortunate. Embracing the survival of the richest, they say, free marketeers promote a bleak, Darwinian world in which the market determines winners and losers. And in such a world, there's no reason to feel sorry for those who get left behind.[16]

But that is simply not the America that most of us know. Merely because the 30 percent coalition attempts to characterize the rest of us that way does not mean it's true. Just as they have attempted to appropriate fairness in America, so they are trying to own compassion. The 70 percent majority must not let this happen. In the same way that the 30 percent's definition of fairness leads to profoundly unfair policies, so their understanding of compassion results in deeply uncompassionate outcomes for the poor.

There are three truths to keep in mind when it comes to compassion for the poor. First, we all want to alleviate poverty. Second, the 30 percent coalition and the 70 percent majority have honest differences about how to go about it. And third, as an empirical matter, only policies and approaches grounded in free enterprise succeed in lifting large groups out of poverty in the long run.[17]

The 30 percent coalition's solution to poverty is simple: redistribution. By shifting wealth from the rich to the poor, they believe they can solve poverty. But this is a failing strategy.

Only free enterprise truly addresses the root causes of poverty. Our solutions are not based on a reslicing of the existing economic pie by government officials and bureaucrats, effectively taking money from the well-off and giving it to the poor through punitive taxation and growing welfare. They are based on an expansion of the pie in ways that will increase everyone's share through policies and a culture that creates incentives for Americans, allows them to tap into the generative power of entrepreneurship, and ultimately lets them earn their own success. Hence our next principle.

We Seek to Stimulate True Prosperity, Not Treat Poverty

In 1974, an economics professor named Muhammad Yunus conducted a study of poverty in a rural village in his native Bangladesh. He found that the local craft workers were skilled and hardworking. But many of them, like the village women who made baskets for a living, could not accumulate enough collateral to secure credit to buy the materials needed to make their small businesses prosper.

Yunus believed the best way to overcome poverty was to unleash individuals' private enterprise. For the basket-makers this could be achieved with just a few dollars in credit—"micro loans" provided by a new kind of bank that required no collateral and charged low rates of interest.[18]

The project had spectacular success, spreading in less than thirty years to nearly 50,000 other villages and across 70 percent of Bangladesh. It helped millions of people escape poverty simply by allowing them to keep the fruits of their own enterprise. In 2006 Yunus was awarded the Nobel Peace Prize, his use of micro-credit lauded as an "important liberating force in societies . . . against repressive social and economic conditions."[19]

Yunus's work truly is a force for good in the world. He showed what we in the free-enterprise movement have always argued—that stimulating prosperity, not simply alleviating poverty, should be the goal for helping the poor and vulnerable.

Study after study of impoverished communities around the world shows that prosperity, not poverty, is the right focus if we want to lift people up. Scholars of international development today know that entrepreneurs enrich themselves but also lift up whole communities around them. That is why Yunus's approach is so much better than traditional government aid, which transfers money from the governments of rich countries to the governments of poor countries for distribution to the impoverished. By concentrating on poverty alleviation (and on governments), traditional aid has often been unresponsive to the needs of people and dismissive of a private sector that is the real means to delivering economic growth and development.[20]

We need not just enterprise programs, however, but healthy cultures and good policy that rewards innovation and enterprise. This means policies that don't penalize success. It also means imbuing market-based development with moral worth by making the cultural case for hard work and enterprise. A huge body of research clearly shows that merely sending foreign aid—the international equivalent of domestic welfare—simply will not work.[21]

So far we have been talking about ways to help the poor in other countries. The same lessons apply to assisting the vulnerable around us in America. Although the extent of poverty here is nothing akin to that in Bangladesh or Africa, we still have communities in need. The official poverty rate in America in 2008 was 13.2 percent, or 39.8 million people. Some 18 percent of American children live in poverty, 8 percent of them in *extreme* poverty. And in 2006, 22.5 percent of the U.S. population endured "asset poverty" (meaning the household's net assets would not cover three months of subsistence living without income).[22]

The question of how to alleviate these problems has occupied American policy-makers for generations. There are two basic sets of solutions.

The first set of solutions are those favored by the 30 percent coalition, who focus on poverty alleviation by transferring monetary resources from richer to poorer. This ideology motivated traditional welfare programs like those introduced during Lyndon B. Johnson's War on Poverty and Great Society programs. Millions were added to the welfare rolls during the late 1960s and early 1970s. The idea was relatively simple: People with jobs paid taxes to the government, and the government developed bureaucracies that bundled up the money for redistribution, thus establishing in loco parentis relationships with the poor.

Welfare programs rely on the idea that poverty is simply a problem of a lack of money. As W. C. Fields put it, "A rich man is nothing but a poor man with money." But the problem is that giving the poor money does not alleviate poverty in the long (or often even the short) run. Instead, it masks cultural conditions by treating the symptoms.

I once interviewed an executive of a large fast-food chain about his hiring practices. I asked him whether he felt bad about creating "dead-end jobs" that paid minimum wage and offered little apparent possibility for advancement. He was surprised and somewhat offended at my question. "The best route to management in this company is by starting in the kitchen at minimum wage," he told me. "Most of our executives started that way. The problem is that so many entry-level employees have terrible work habits. They create their own dead ends."

In a country such as the United States, it is hard to argue that opportunity does not exist. But it's not hard to argue that certain people lack the skills and abilities to exploit opportunities. I am not talking about the infirm and mentally ill, but the masses of able-bodied citizens stuck in cycles of poverty and dependence. They have a cultural barrier to work and enterprise. This barrier is strengthened by simple income redistribution, which divorces money from earned success and provides a short-term solution at best.

Because they do not strengthen culture and reinforce values, American welfare programs have spectacularly failed to end poverty. As Ronald Reagan put it in his 1988 State of the Union Address, "My friends, some years ago the federal government declared war on poverty, and poverty won." In 1970 the total number of welfare recipients in America was 8.5 million, of whom 6.2 million were children. By 1996 total recipients had increased to 12.3 million, of whom 8.5 million were children. Welfare rolls increased not just in actual numbers, but as a percentage of the population.[23]

Occasionally, we get things right, though. Major reform improved the American welfare system in 1996. That year, new legislation reduced the dangers of dependency on the system by limiting the length of time a person could receive support and by requiring those receiving benefits to work. Many in the 30 percent coalition were outraged. One prominent children's advocate called the law an "outrage . . . that will hurt and impoverish millions of American children." Further, she predicted that it would "leave a moral blot on . . . our nation that will never be forgotten." But in the first seven years of the new law, the U.S. poverty rate actually fell from 13.7 percent to 12.5 percent, and it did so during a time of economic recession. Some 4.7 million Americans moved from welfare dependency to self-sufficiency within three years. Refocusing welfare from alleviating poverty to expecting work had rescued millions of Americans.[24]

Poverty-based solutions don't work. They are also unethical because, as we have seen, work—and the success that stems from work (rather than handouts)—is essential to human flourishing. Redistributive government welfare programs rob the poor of their chance for earned success and their inalienable right to the pursuit of happiness.[25]

Prosperity-based solutions are the answer. This means policies that stimulate entrepreneurship and jobs. Not make-work jobs from the government, but jobs that fill a need for entrepreneurs dedicated to creating real value. And the best thing policymakers can do is allow these entrepreneurs to keep more of the money they earn, invest in their businesses, and expand their operations. This is not ideology but the conclusion of volumes of research, into which the endnotes of this book provide an introduction.[26]

In his January 2010 State of the Union Address, President Obama made a step in the right direction when he proposed incentives to help small businesses. This is encouraging—as long as it is not purely tactical, an attempt to score political points or a tool to pick winners and losers in the private economy. To prove that it is indeed a genuine attempt to fuel honest job growth and entrepreneurship, the president should move beyond the rhetoric to real policy proposals to help all business owners: across-the-board tax cuts on corporate income, capital gains, and dividends. And this should be absolutely central to the aspiring politicians' offerings to America in the months and years ahead.

These ideas come with a distinct "Made in the U.S.A." stamp. They ring with the sentiment of our Founding Fathers, whose gift to us was the system that let us pursue our happiness. But these ideas have a more universal application, too, which leads us to our next principle.

America Can and Should Be a Gift to the World

We are accustomed to hearing foreigners say that America is exploitative—a destructive force around the globe. But how many Americans agree with this sort of assessment?

The breakdown of Americans' support of America's actions on the world stage, pro and con, is—no surprise—approximately 70 percent and 30 percent, respectively. A 2006 survey asked which statement people agreed with more: (a) America's power is generally a force for good in the world; or (b) power generally does more harm than good when we act abroad. Sixty-four percent chose (a), whereas 32 percent chose (b). Apologizing for America is a preoccupation of the 30 percent coalition. This minority culture believes that we exploit other countries economically, use too much of the world's resources, infect noble lands with capitalism, and use our military power to impose our will abroad.[27]

The rest of us are offended at the notion that we should apologize for America. Nearly 70 percent believe that our country does more good than harm. Of course, our public opinion alone does not in itself prove that we are a force for good in the world. Just because we believe it doesn't make it so. After all, it's possible that majorities in the Soviet Union or in Nazi Germany also felt their countries were forces for good (had they ever been asked what they thought, that is).

But the evidence is clear: Our world would be a poorer and less secure place today but for the influence of the United States. As an engine of freedom, opportunity, and enterprise internationally, America truly has been a gift to the world over the generations.

Take free trade, for example—much maligned by the international left wing (and some parts of the right). Trade has played a critical part in the recovering U.S. economy since the fall of 2009. It has similarly played an unlauded role in the well-being of the world over the last half century and more. The volume of merchandise traded in 2005, for instance, was 27 times greater than the trade levels in 1950. This has had an overwhelmingly beneficial effect on the world economy: World output in that same period increased by a factor of eight, increasing prosperity all around poorer parts of the globe. Of course, you would never know this by watching and listening to activists protesting against globalization and free enterprise.[28]

According to the World Bank, China alone has accounted for more than 75 percent of poverty reduction in the entire developing world over the past two decades, in part by trading with America. Indeed, from 1990 to 2006 the value of Chinese exports to the United States increased by more than 1,000 percent in inflation-adjusted terms. This represents, literally, millions of export-fueled jobs. All that Chinese stuff you buy is giving someone in China a means to support his or her family.[29]

But trade does more than promote economic growth and prosperity. U.S. free trade agreements also help countries solidify economic and governance reforms. Trade helps countries share ideas. It fosters cross-cultural understanding and creates disincentives to fight. Fueled by America, free trade is a way to foster the development of democracy and civil society worldwide.[30]

To be sure, not every free-trading, capitalistic country is an open, democratic regime. Places like Dubai and Singapore have progress to make on these fronts by American standards. But a lack of free trade and capitalism is a classic characteristic of nondemocratic governance. Witness how authoritarian regimes such as Venezuela under Hugo Chávez feel compelled to jettison institutions of free enterprise as they tighten social control.

Despite the evidence, the leaders of the 30 percent coalition do not believe that America is a gift to the world. So it is no surprise that they have shown ambivalence toward trade with other countries. We have violated the North American Free Trade Agreement (NAFTA) with Mexico by failing to allow entry of Mexican trucks into the United States. We have slapped tariffs on Chinese tires for no reason other than the appeasement of American labor unions. And we have failed to pursue agreements already in progress with such allies as Colombia and Panama.[31]

This is not just poor economic policy. It is evidence of the belief that America is not a gift to the world.

So far my focus has been almost entirely on free enterprise. But those who reject the idea that America is a gift to the world often—perhaps usually—point to military issues.

Radicals on the left have always been hostile to American military efforts. Many in academia openly state that the "real" war criminals in the past decade are George Bush and Dick Cheney, not Saddam Hussein and Osama bin Laden. These are fringe views. More mainstream is the question of whether America's military investment is consistent with the 70 percent majority's support for free-enterprise culture. Although this is not a book about foreign policy, advocates of our system need to be willing and able to take on this issue directly.[32]

The claim that American militarism is to blame for the world's woes is indefensible. In World War I American military strength brought to an end the bloodiest, costliest war that had ever been waged up until that point in history. In World War II, which began for the United States when the Japanese attacked Pearl Harbor and Germany declared war on us, the American nation mobilized to end the twin evils of Japanese militarism and Nazism—and converted Japan and Germany into prosperous, free nations. And through victory in the Cold War, won without a direct engagement of troops, America gave freedom to hundreds of millions of people previously in the shackles of Soviet communism.

In the post–Cold War world, America has continued its role of liberator and deliverer of free-enterprise values. During the conflict in Kosovo in 1999, U.S. forces intervened to save the lives of Muslim civilians and laid the groundwork for several new market economies. And in Iraq in 2003, the U.S.-led coalition overthrew a brutal dictator and (despite poor execution and strategy for several years) now appears to have set that nation on the road to freedom. In the wake of the bombing of the World Trade Center in September 2001, America led a coalition of nations to destroy al-Qaeda in Afghanistan and overthrow the oppressive Taliban regime, a sect so tyrannical in its rule that it sought to outlaw everything from kite-flying to singing.[33]

America can and does make mistakes. It is naive to say we are perfect around the world. We are not. We don't yet know precisely how Afghanistan and Iraq will turn out, and it is completely reasonable to question whether these military engagements were always appropriately executed. But in general, a world without the American military legacy would be poorer and less free.

Of course, America's military role in the world does come at a tremendous cost, human as well as financial. Some critics on both the left and right lambast our "interventionist" foreign policy for the billions it has cost in taxpayer dollars, let alone American lives. And in this they see an opportunity to skewer traditional conservatives, whom they accuse of trying to restrain domestic government spending while showing no such restraint in defense spending.

But as most Americans understand, the free-enterprise movement is not the "no-government" movement. Free enterprise requires property rights and police, so that what is rightfully yours cannot be taken away by a criminal. Of course, this imposes your values on the criminal who wants your wallet, and it also costs money. But that is not objectionable.

Military intervention around the world is more complicated than police protection at home, and we need an ongoing debate about our military's role in the world. But the protective role of military spending cannot be compared with enterprise-wrecking government boondoggles like car company bailouts. And the fact that most people see the military in a positive light and support our activities abroad is not philosophically inconsistent to a people who agree that American free enterprise can and should be a gift to the world.

So where does all this leave the free-enterprise movement in America? How can the 70 percent majority find leadership that dependably expresses our values? In a nutshell, how do we win?

In Washington, DC, a lot of people think they know the answer. They say what is needed are telegenic candidates, dirty tricks, and a lot of campaign money. They know exactly how many seats "we" need to gain in the next election, which politicians from the other party are vulnerable, and how the White House can be won. In other words, they talk about tactics, political parties, and power. This is an error.

What Truly Matters Is Principle, Not Political Power

Our final principle is a difficult one—for everyone. In America the pursuit of political power at the expense of principle has been ruinous for both of our main political parties. It has destroyed public confidence.

Today, the general public believes that politicians can't be trusted. The World Economic Forum's *Global Competitiveness Report, 2009–2010* polled citizens around the world on the following question: "On a scale of 1 to 7, how would you rate the level of public trust in the ethical standards of politicians in your country?" The United States placed a mediocre 43rd in the world, with a rating of 3.4.[34]

Confidence in politicians in America is now as low as it was in the era of Watergate. A December 2010 Gallup poll reveals an approval rating for Congress of just 13 percent. According to the General Social Survey, those with a "great deal of confidence" in the executive branch fell from 17 percent of Americans in 1988 to 11 percent in 2008. During that same time period, confidence in the courts went from 37 percent to 32 percent.[35]

The one public institution that did see a rise in public confidence levels was the military. Over the 20-year period, confidence in the U.S. military rose from 36 percent of Americans to 52 percent. Notably, however, the confidence is not evenly shared between left and right. While 73 percent of those who described themselves as "extremely conservative" say they have a great deal of confidence in the military, only 32 percent of "extremely liberal" Americans share this view.[36] The popular lack of trust in government doesn't indicate that Americans are just a suspicious lot. According to Gallup, 73 percent of Americans say they trust their fellow citizens' judgments about the issues facing the nation. Americans may not have widespread faith in their government, but they do believe in themselves and in each other.[37]

So why should Americans not trust government? After all, they were the ones who put our nation's leaders into office. "Buyer's remorse" aside, I believe that what matters most to the American people is the commitment to principle and not the exercise of political power. And this is a truth that many of our current politicians and pundits have failed to learn.

Let's look in particular at the political party that had most to learn in the wake of the 2008 election—the losers. As soon as the crushing defeat in the November 2008 elections was official, the Republican excuses began to fly, and plans were quickly hatched to win back power, not principle. In some

Republican circles, the debate has focused on which demographic groups the party should be targeting. Others on the right are zeroing in on the need to generate party enthusiasm, good organization, and high turnout. Or the need to triangulate Evangelicals. Or to expand the base. Or how the party can best hold onto the working-class vote. Or how it should "go upscale."

Not enough have taken the time to look back on the real reasons the Republicans lost in 2008. John McCain lost primarily because of the recession and the fact that Republicans had no narrative for the crisis (not even a false one like the Democrats). But Americans also saw that the GOP had no principled solutions for America.

The truth is that the American electorate did not repudiate free enterprise or conservative principles in November 2008. Rather, it punished an unprincipled Republican party. American politics had not become too conservative for the American appetite. Rather, American politics had strayed too far from its free-enterprise values.

Unprincipled behavior destroyed Republicans' public approval. A Harris Poll conducted in October 2001 found that 67 percent of Americans believed congressional Republicans were doing a good job. By February 2004 it was 40 percent. By September 2008 public approval had dipped to 22 percent.[38]

Misunderstanding this point will guarantee future defeat for Republicans. Should we care? Ideally, no, if we had a Democratic party that respected the values of the 70 percent majority. As a political independent, I would gladly vote for any political party dedicated to limited government and entrepreneurship.

Unfortunately, the Democrats continue to lurch to the left, with our free-enterprise system increasingly thrown to the tender mercies of such people as Harry Reid and Barney Frank. Between Republican chaos and Democratic leftism, many Americans feel they have had no place to go.

America needs leaders as committed as we are to expanding liberty, increasing individual opportunity, and defending free enterprise. In short, we need leaders committed to the source of our flourishing and the bedrock of our culture.

This is not wishful thinking. There are ways that it can actually happen. Political turmoil can lead to renewal, and the challenges of this new culture war can give us what we need to remobilize and reassert our core principles. As one old saying goes, "When power is withdrawn, desperate men turn to principle."

In 1964 the proponents of free enterprise suffered large-scale political defeat, and great soul-searching ensued. A widespread belief took hold at the time that the American people had permanently turned away from free market values. Ronald Reagan rejected this notion out of hand. They had lost a battle in 1964 but not the war.[39]

Throughout the 1970s, Reagan talked about principles—principles like those laid out here. "We represent the forgotten American," he told the nation, "that simple soul who goes to work, bucks for a raise, takes out insurance, pays for his kids' schooling, contributes to his church and charity, and knows there just 'ain't no such thing as a free lunch.'" These ruminations sound positively subversive today, in the midst of government bailouts for almost every deadbeat on Wall Street and Main Street. But we all know where Reagan's musings ended up: with him in the White House, guiding our nation to greater freedom, opportunity, and strength than it had seen in decades.

The 2008 election, then, was perhaps exactly what America needed. There is a very real threat before us that the 30 percent coalition may transform our great nation forever. One can only hope that this threat will clear our thinking enough to bring forth leaders with our principles at heart and the ideas to match. If principle triumphs over the mere quest for political power, perhaps the four other core principles of the free-enterprise movement will emerge anew. And America will be the stronger for it.

Notes

Introduction

1. Gallup, June 2010,
   www.gallup.com/poll/File/141104/Tea_Party_Support_Jul
   y_2_2010.pdf.

2. Gallup, December 2010,
   www.gallup.com/poll/145238/Congress-Job-Approval
   -Rating-Worst-Gallup-History.aspx.

3. A March 2010 *USA Today*/Gallup poll finds that Tea
   Partiers are generally mainstream in their demographics,
   representative of the public at large in terms of age, education, and employment. It also finds that 28 percent of
   American adults call themselves Tea Party supporters.

   www.gallup.com/poll/127181/tea-partiers-fairly-
   mainstream-demographics.aspx,

   www.politicsdaily.com/2009/08/06/harry-reid-health-care
   -protests-astroturf-not-grass-roots/.

4. Resurgent Republic, National Survey of Registered Voters,
   January 12–16, 2011.

Chapter One

1. See Michael Novak, *The Spirit of Democratic Capitalism* (Lanham, MD: Madison Books, 1991) and Charles Murray, "The Happiness of the People," 2009 Irving Kristol Lecture, American Enterprise Institute for Public Policy Research.

2. Thomas Jefferson, First Inaugural Address, March 4, 1801. The Avalon Project at Yale Law School, http://avalon.law.yale.edu/19th_century/jefinaul.asp; Heritage Research Institute, www.heritageresearchinstitute.org/founders.html.

3. Alexis de Tocqueville, *Democracy in America* (London: Saunders and Otley, 1835–1840).

4. Ibid.

5. Andrew Kohut and Bruce Stokes, *America Against the World: How We Are Different and Why We Are Disliked* (New York: Henry Holt, 2006).

6. The acclaimed economist Joseph Schumpeter described entrepreneurship in 1934 the following way: "First of all there is the dream and the will to found a private kingdom, usually, though not necessarily, also a dynasty . . . The financial result is a secondary consideration, or, at all events, mainly valued as an index of success and as a symptom of victory, the displaying of which very often is more important as a motive of large expenditure than the wish for the consumers' goods themselves. . . . Finally, there is the joy of creating, of getting things done, or simply of exercising one's energy and ingenuity. . . . Our type seeks out difficulties, changes in order to

change, delights in ventures." J. A. Schumpeter (trans. R. Opie), *The Theory of Economic Development* (Cambridge, MA: Harvard University Press, 1934), 93–94.

7. Finally, you now have evidence that your unhappiness is your parents' fault. See David Lykken and Auke Tellegen, "Happiness Is a Stochastic Phenomenon," *Psychological Science* 7, no. 3 (1996); see John D. Gartner, *The Hypomanic Edge. The Link Between (a Little) Craziness and (a Lot of) Success in America* (New York: Simon & Schuster, 2005).

8. David Brooks, "The Protocol Society," *New York Times*, December 22, 2009. www.nytimes.com/2009/12/22/opinion/22brooks.html.

9. Gallup News Service, "Capitalism, Business and Government Regulation," survey conducted January 26–27, 2010.

10. http://people-press.org/reports/pdf/498.pdf.

11. Tax Foundation, "How Do Americans Feel About Taxes Today?" Special Report, April 2009, www.taxfoundation.org/files/sr166.pdf.

12. FOX News Poll/Opinion Dynamics, March 5, 2009, www.foxnews.com/projects/pdf/030509_Poll.pdf.

13. Ayres, McHenry & Associates (AM&A), Resurgent Republic National Survey of Registered Voters, April 13–16, 2009, www.resurgentrepublic.com/system/assets/6/original/RR_Presentation.pdf. Curtis S. Dubay, "Obama's 2011 Budget Tax Hikes Contradict Focus on Job Creation," *Wall Street Journal*, February 5, 2010, http://online.wsj.com/article/SB10001424052748704533204575047720489119784.html.

14. ABC News/*Washington Post* Poll, March 2009: "Would you describe yourself as angry or not angry about the role . . . large business corporations have played in the economic situation?" (68 percent angry, 31 percent not angry, 1 percent no opinion). Data provided by the Roper Center for Public Opinion Research, University of Connecticut.

15. Pew Research Center for the People & the Press, 2009 Values Survey, http://people-press.org/reports/question-naires/517.pdf.

16. Ibid.; Gallup News Service, "Capitalism, Business and Government Regulation," January 26–27, 2010.

17. Lydia Saad, "Labor Unions See Sharp Slide in U.S. Public Support," September 3, 2009, www.gallup.com/poll/122744/Labor-Unions-Sharp-Slide-Public-Support.aspx?CSTS=alert#1; Gallup News Service, "Americans Leery of Too Much Government Regulation of Business," February 2, 2010, www.gallup.com/poll/125468/americans-leery-govt-regu-lation-business.aspx.

18. James R. Hagerty, "Fannie and Freddie to Aid Mortgage Banks," *Wall Street Journal*, October 8, 2009, http://online.wsj.com/article/SB125486796534968995.html.

19. Pew Charitable Trusts, Economic Mobility Project, January 2009, www.economicmobility.org/poll2009/tool_1.

20. AM&A, Resurgent Republic National Survey of Registered Voters, April 13–16, 2009. Democrats were more equally divided on this question (at 44 percent and 48 percent, respectively).

21. James A. Davis, Tom W. Smith, and Peter V. Marsden, *General Social Surveys, 1972–2006* (Storrs, CT: Roper Center for Public Opinion Research, University of Connecticut, 2006).

22. CBS/*New York Times* poll, February 5–10, 2010; Survey by Cable News Network and Opinion Research Corporation, December 19–21, 2008. Retrieved June 3, 2009, from the iPOLL Databank, The Roper Center for Public Opinion Research, University of Connecticut, www.roper-center.uconn.edu/ipoll.html.

23. Using the General Social Survey, Charles Murray calculates this concentration by splitting people up by income, education, and occupation, and then looking at the logit-fitted percentage calling themselves "liberal" or "very liberal" minus those who say they are "conservative" or "very conservative." Murray's analysis focuses on the white population. Nonwhites are more likely to call themselves "very liberal." ("The White House and the Pauline Kael Syndrome," by Charles Murray, *The Enterprise Blog*, August 25, 2009, http://blog.american.com/?p=4259.). Whereas "liberal" and "conservative" do not map onto attitudes about free enterprise perfectly, they do so extremely well. Take the issue of government income redistribution, for example. In 2005, when asked, "Should government do more to try to reduce inequality?" 84 percent of liberals said yes, versus just 25 percent of conservatives. The Maxwell Poll (2005), Civic Engagement and Inequality, October 2005, [merged data set], www1.maxwell.syr.edu/campbell/programs/Merged_Data_Set/.

24. Bob Young, "Obama's Big-Time Fumble at ASU," *Arizona Republic*, May 17, 2009,

www.azcentral.com/sports/asu/articles/2009/05/17/20090
517spt-p2mainyoung.html. See also John Ward, "Parsing
Obama's view of self-interest and culture," *Washington
Times*, May 14, 2009, www.washingtontimes.com/
weblogs/potus-notes/2009/may/14/parsing-obamas
-view-of-self-interest-and-culture/.

25. The GSS data show that whereas 43 percent of professors
self-identify as "liberal," only 14 percent of workers in
general do
(www.nytimes.com/imagepages/2010/01/18/arts/18liberal
-2.html). Other numbers cited in George F. Will, "Academia, Stuck to the Left," *Washington Post*, November 28,
2004, www.washingtonpost.com/wp-dyn/articles/
A15606–2004Nov26.html.

26. Daniel B. Klein and Andrew Western, "How Many
Democrats per Republican at UC-Berkeley and Stanford?
Voter Registration Data Across 23 Academic
Departments," *Scandinavian Working Papers in Econom-
ics*, http://swopec.hhs.se/ratioi/abs/ratioi0054.htm; Daniel
B. Klein and Charlotta Stern, "Is There a Free-Market
Economist in the House? The Policy Views of American
Economic Association Members," *American Journal of
Economics and Sociology*, 66, no. 2 (2007),
www.gmu.edu/departments/economics/klein/PdfPapers/
Klein-Stern%20AJES%202007.pdf.

27. Media Research Center, "Media Bias 101,"
www.mrc.org/static/uploads/MediaBias101.pdf.

28. Mike Collett-White, "'Capitalism Is Evil,' Says New
Michael Moore Film," Reuters, September 6, 2009,
www.reuters.com/article/lifestyleMolt/idUSTRE5850F320
090906.

29. OpenSecrets.org, "TV/Movies/Music: Long-Term Contribution Trends," www.opensecrets.org/industries/indus.php?ind=B02; Mike Dorning and Christi Parsons, "Hollywood: Democrats' Land of Plenty," *Chicago Tribune*, February 21, 2007, www.chicagotribune.com/news/nationworld/chi-0702210200feb21,0,1702672.story; "Ideology at Work," *New York Times*, January 18, 2010, www.nytimes.com/imagepages/2010/01/18/arts/18liberal-2.html.

30. Social Capital Community Benchmark Survey, 2000.

31. Rasmussen Reports, "Just 53% Say Capitalism Better Than Socialism," April 9, 2009, www.rasmussenreports.com/public_content/politics/general_politics/just_53_say_capitalism_better_than_socialism; Gallup News Service, "Capitalism, Business and Government Regulation," conducted January 26–27, 2010.

32. CNNPolitics.com, Election Center 2008, http://www.cnn.com/ELECTION/2008/results/polls/.

33. The program was created by the Democrats in Congress in 2007 but reannounced by the president in 2009.

34. "The Government Pay Bonus," by Andrew G. Biggs and Jason Richwine, *Wall Street Journal*, July 6, 2010, www.aei.org/article/102263.

35. IRS Statistics of Income, "Table 1. Returns with Positive Adjusted Gross Income," www.irs.gov/pub/irs-soi/06in01etr.xls, http://www.irs.gov/pub/irs-soi/07in01etr.xls, and author's calculations.

36. Tax Foundation, "How Do Americans Feel About Taxes Today? Tax Foundation's 2009 Survey of U.S. Attitudes on

Taxes, Government Spending and Wealth Distribution,"
April 2009, No. 166,
www.taxfoundation.org/files/sr166.pdf.

37. Tax Policy Center, "Tax Units with Zero or Negative
Income Tax Liability, 2009–2019," accessed June 24,
2009,
www.taxpolicycenter.org/numbers/displayatab.cfm?DocID
=2408; Tax Policy Center, www.taxpolicycenter.org/
numbers/displayatab.cfm?Docid=1973&DocTypeID=7;
Adam Lerrick "Obama and the Tax Tipping Point," *Wall
Street Journal,* October 22, 2008,
http://online.wsj.com/article/SB12246323104855
6587.html.

38. Thomas Jefferson, letter to E. Carrington, May 27, 1788.

39. See the federal budget data:
www.whitehouse.gov/omb/budget/fy2010/assets/
hist04z1.xls.

40. Congressional Budget Office, estimates for the Medicare
Modernization Act,
www.cbo.gov/doc.cfm?index=6139&type=0.

41. David Kirkpatrick, "Question of Timing on Bush's Push
on Earmarks," *New York Times,* January 29, 2008,
www.nytimes.com/2008/01/29/washington/
29earmark.html.

42. Chris Edwards, Cato Institute, Tax & Budget Bulletin,
August 2005, www.cato.org/pubs/tbb/tbb-0508-24.pdf.

Chapter Two

1. Iowa Electronic Markets,
   www.biz.uiowa.edu/iem/index.cfm.

2. CNN ElectionCenter2008,
   http://www.cnn.com/ELECTION/2008/results/president/
   United States Presidential Election Results, www.uselec-
   tionatlas.org/RESULTS/index.html.

3. "A 40-Year Wish List," *Wall Street Journal*, January 28,
   2009, http://online.wsj.com/article/SB1233104665145
   22309.html.

4. Alex Pollock, "Ten Thoughts on the Causes of the Bubble
   and Bust," *American Spectator*, May 29, 2009, http://
   spectator.org/archives/2009/05/29/ten-thoughts-on
   -the-causes-of/print; "Minutes of the Federal Open Market Committee," Board of Governors of the Federal
   Reserve System, June 24–25, 2008,
   www.federalreserve.gov/monetarypolicy/fomcminutes2008
   0625ep.htm.

5. "Update 1–Bush: U.S. Economy Not in Recession, in
   Slowdown," Reuters, April 22, 2008,
   www.reuters.com/article/idUSN2231537320080422;
   Karen Tumulty, "McCain: Selling an Economic Policy,"
   Time.com, July 10, 2008, www.time.com/time/politics/
   article/0,8599,1821470,00.html#ixzz0ZOd9zlSb; Michael
   Cooper, "McCain Adviser Refers to 'Nation of Whiners,'"
   New York Times, www.nytimes.com/2008/07/11/us/
   politics/11campaign.html.

6. The DJIA closed September 2, 2008, at 11,516.92; the
   close on October 27, 2008, was 8,175.77, a 29 percent

decline. See "Historical Prices," Yahoo! Finance,
http://finance.yahoo.com/q/hp?s=^DJI&a=08&b=1&c=2
008&d=10&e=5&f=2008&g=d.

7. Bureau of Economic Analysis, "Table 2.1. Personal
Income and Its Disposition," www.bea.gov/national/
nipaweb/TableView.asp?SelectedTable=58&ViewSeries=N
O&Java=no&Request3Place=N&3Place=N&FromView=Y
ES&Freq=Qtr&FirstYear=1929&LastYear=2009&3Place=
N&Update=Update&JavaBox=no#Mid; Bureau of Labor
Statistics, "The Employment Situation–December 2009,"
http://tsisolution.com/whats-new/wp-content/uploads/
2010/01/December-2009-Unemployment-Situation.pdf;
Bureau of Labor Statistics, http://data.bls.gov/cgi-bin/
surveymost; Shamim Adam, "Global Financial Assets Lost
$50 Trillion Last Year, ADB Says," March 9, 2009,
Bloomberg.com,
www.bloomberg.com/apps/news?pid=newsarchive&sid=
aZ1kcJ7y3LDM.

8. According to the Case-Shiller 20-city composite home
price index, Standard & Poors, S&P/Case-Shiller Home
Price Indices, www.standardandpoors.com/indices/sp
-case-shiller-home-price-indices/en/us/%3FindexId=
spusa-cashpidff–p-us––.

9. "Fundamental Question: Is Economy Really OK?" Associated Press, September 17, 2008, www.msnbc.msn.com/id/
26744322/ns/business-stocks_and_economy//; Jennifer
Loven, "Bush Says Economy Strong Enough to Handle
Turmoil," Associated Press, www.usatoday.com/news/
topstories/2008–09–15–590281267_x.htm.

10. Jonathan Martin and Carol E. Lee, "Obama to GOP:
'I Won,'" *Politico*, January 23, 2009,
www.politico.com/news/stories/0109/17862.html.

11. "The Stimulus Advances," *New York Times*, January 28, 2009, www.nytimes.com/2009/01/29/opinion/29thu1.html; "Getting Tough in Washington," *New York Times*, February 5, 2009, www.nytimes.com/2009/02/06/opinion/06fri1.html?_r=2&ref=opinion%20.

12. Mark Pittman and Bob Ivry, "Financial Rescue Nears GDP as Pledges Top $12.8 Trillion," Bloomberg.com, March 31, 2009, www.bloomberg.com/apps/news?pid=20601087&sid=armOzfkwtCA4; Board of Governors of the Federal Reserve System, "Mortgage Debt Outstanding," December 2009, www.federalreserve.gov/econresdata/releases/mortoutstand/current.htm.

13. John Meacham and Evan Thomas. "We Are All Socialists Now," *Newsweek*, February 7, 2009, www.newsweek.com/id/183663.

14. Craig Whitlock. "E.U. President Blasts U.S. Spending," *Washington Post*, March 26, 2009, www.washingtonpost.com/wp-dyn/content/article/2009/03/25/AR2009032502074.html; "China's Leader Says He Is 'Worried' Over U.S. Treasuries," *New York Times*, March 13, 2009, www.nytimes.com/2009/03/14/world/asia/14china.html.

15. "'Immediate Action' Needed, Bush Says," The CNN Wire, September 2008, http://cnnwire.blogs.cnn.com/2008/09/24/immediate-action-needed-bush-says/; Matthew Benjamin and Rich Miller, "Conservatives Mourn White House's 'Abandoning' Reagan Legacy," Bloomberg.com, www.bloomberg.com/apps/news?pid=washingtonstory&sid=aq1bXzDN.GlY; "Road to Stability," FinancialStability.gov, July 6, 2009, www.financialstability.gov/roadtostability/programs.htm; "The Troubled Assets Relief Program: Report on Transactions Through

December 31, 2008," A CBO Report, January 2009,
www.cbo.gov/ftpdocs/99xx/doc9961/01
-16-TARP.pdf.

16. David Rogers and Mike Allen, "Bush Announces $17.4
Billion Auto Bailout," December 19, 2008,
www.politico.com/news/stories/1208/16740.html.

17. You could certainly argue that there was insufficient regulation of Fannie and Freddie, but in this case it was the
Bush administration that proposed a strong GSE regulator
and congressional Democrats who rejected it.

18. While it was founded as a New Deal government agency
in 1938, Fannie Mae was rechartered by Congress in 1968
and converted into a private, shareholder-owned corporation whose operations were backed by the federal
government. Freddie Mac was chartered by Congress in
1970 for much the same reason. Note that the 1968 reor-
ganization of Fannie was an effort to improve the federal
balance sheet by getting loan guarantees off the books. So
while the ostensible purpose of the GSEs was to provide
liquidity by securitizing mortgages, the direct impulse was
simply a desire to hide fiscal reality.

19. The original Federal Reserve Bank of Boston study that
claimed widespread discrimination in mortgage lending,
and was cited as support for a more active Community
Reinvestment Act, was actually later debunked. See Alicia
H. Munnell, Lynn E. Browne, James McEneaney, and
Geoffrey M. B. Tootell, "Mortgage Lending in Boston:
Interpreting HMDA Data," Federal Reserve Bank of
Boston, Working Paper, October 1992,
www.bos.frb.org/economic/wp/wp1992/wp92_7.htm.

20. Subprime loans are the riskiest, typically made to borrowers with blemished credit histories ranging from payment delinquency to bankruptcy. Alt-A, or Alternative A-paper, loans usually have less credit risk than subprime but more than prime, or A-paper. Alt-A mortgages are usually made when borrowers have incomplete documentation and lower credit scores. The price of both kinds of loan (slightly higher rates) reflects the risk assumed by the lender.

21. Peter Wallison, "The True Origins of This Financial Crisis," *American Spectator*, February 2009, http:// spectator.org/archives/2009/02/06/the-true-origins -of-this-finan/.

22. Peter Wallison and Charles Calomiris, "The Last Trillion-Dollar Commitment: The Destruction of Fannie Mae and Freddie Mac," *Financial Services Outlook*, September 2008, www.aei.org/docLib/20080930_Binder1.pdf.

23. Ibid. Peter Wallison and Charles Calomiris. "The Last Trillion-Dollar Commitment: The Destruction of Fannie Mae and Freddie Mac," AEI *Financial Services Outlook*, September 2008, www.aei.org/outlook/28704.

24. James Gwartney, David Macpherson, Russell Sobel, and Richard Stroup, "The Economic Crisis of 2008: Cause and Aftermath," www.commonsenseeconomics.com/ Activities/Crisis/CSE.Housing%20Crisis.PPT.pdf.

25. As Wall Street financier Paul Singer lamented, "Most global financial institutions built highly leveraged balance sheets—sometimes as high as 30 to 1—that were stuffed with risky assets." Paul Singer, "Free-Marketeers Should Welcome Some Regulation," *Wall Street Journal*, April 3,

2009, http://online.wsj.com/article/SB1238718483448
84871.html.

26. Julia Kollewe, "Write-Downs of Largest Banks Reach
$247bn," *The Guardian*, July 29, 2008,
www.guardian.co.uk/business/2008/jul/29/creditcrunch.
MBSs were given investment-grade credit rating, which
further fueled their demand. When the credit rating was
lowered, firms had to lower their value on their books and
sell stock to maintain capital ratios.

27. Emily Parker, "Corporate Hell-Raiser," *Wall Street Journal*, November 15, 2008, http://online.wsj.com/article/
SB122670709684029837.html.

28. Kevin Hassett, "How the Democrats Created the Financial
Crisis: Kevin Hassett," Bloomberg.com, September 22,
2008, www.bloomberg.com/apps/news?pid=
newsarchive&sid=aSKSoiNbnQY0.

29. Lindsay Renick Mayer, "Update: Fannie Mae and Freddie
Mac Invest in Lawmakers," Open Secrets Center for
Responsive Politics, September 11, 2008,
www.opensecrets.org/news/2008/09/update-fannie
-mae-and-freddie.html.

30. David Goldman, "CNNMoney.com's Bailout Tracker,"
http://money.cnn.com/news/storysupplement/economy/ba
ilouttracker/index.html; "U.S. Treasury Ends Cap on Fannie, Freddie Lifeline for 3 Years," by Rebecca Christie and
Jody Shenn, Bloomberg.com,
www.bloomberg.com/apps/news?pid=20601087&sid=abT
VUSp9zbAY&pos=1.

31. "In U.S., 35% Would Rather Work for Gov't Than for
Business," Gallup, January 29, 2010,

www.gallup.com/poll/125426/in-u.s.-35-rather-work-govt-than-business.aspx.

32. "Deregulation Under Bush 43: Myths and Realities," AEI Center for Regulatory and Market Studies, May 6, 2009; Veronique de Rugy, "The Incredible Growth of the Regulators' Budget," Mercatus Working Papers, September 16, 2008.

33. "Author Claims 20-Year Affair with Madoff," August 15, 2009, www.cbsnews.com/stories/2009/08/15/national/main5244037.shtml.

34. Lorena Mongelli and Dan Mangan, "The SEC Watchdog Who Missed Madoff," *New York Post*, January 7, 2009, www.nypost.com/p/news/business/item_IbjeXQwwTt0whX l6ojz3oJ/1.

35. "SEC Pummeled as Madoff Whistleblower Testifies," Reuters UK, February 5, 2009, http://uk.reuters.com/article/pensionsNews/idUKLNE51402Q20090205.

36. nancialstability.gov/docs/regs/FinalReport_web.pdf.

37. In 2002, Nobel laureate Joseph Stiglitz coauthored a paper that claimed the chance of a Fannie-Freddie meltdown was "effectively zero." According to the paper, "This analysis shows that, based on historical data, the probability of a shock as severe as embodied in the risk-based capital standard is substantially less than one in 500,000—and may be smaller than one in three million. Given the low probability of the stress test shock occurring, and assuming that Fannie Mae and Freddie Mac hold sufficient capital to withstand that shock, the exposure of the government to the risk that the GSEs will become insolvent appears quite low." Joseph E. Stiglitz, Jonathan

M. Orszag, and Peter R. Orszag, "Implications of the New
Fannie Mae and Freddie Mac Risk-Based Capital
Standard," *Fannie Mae Papers* 1, no. 2, March 2002,
http://doc.laissez-faire.eu/stiglitz_amoureux_de_fannie
_mae.pdf; Board of Governors of the Federal Reserve Sys-
tem, "Minutes of the Federal Open Market Committee,"
October 28–29, 2008, www.federalreserve.gov/monetary-
policy/fomcminutes20081029ep.htm; Reid Wilson,
"Biden Admits Administration 'Misread' Economy," *The
Hill*, July 5, 2009, http://thehill.com/homenews/
administration/49378-biden-admits-administration
-misread-economy.

38. Bloomberg L. P. "U.S. Economic Forecasts: Bloomberg
Monthly Survey." May 2–8, 2008. (Retrieved June 10,
2009, from Bloomberg database.)

39. Another beef against Cash for Clunkers was that it basically destroyed a ton of usable wealth; the difference
between the scrap value of the car and what it could have
been sold for was essentially destroyed, so to the degree
the program did raise GDP (which is questionable), it did
it in the same way that Hurricane Katrina did: destroy
capital, which isn't counted, but count the production of
replacements toward GDP growth.

40. Vincent Fernanco, "70% of the Q3 GDP Growth Was Cash
for Clunkers," *Business Insider*, December 22, 2009,
www.businessinsider.com/70-of-the-gdp-growth-was-cash
-for-clunkers-2009–12; Catherine Clifford, "Cash for
Clunkers Coming Soon," CNNMoney.com, June 24, 2009,
http://money.cnn.com/2009/06/19/news/economy/cash
_for_clunkers/index.htm.

41. Kevin Hassett, "Toddlers Buy Houses When Stimulus Trumps Reason," Bloomberg.com, October 26, 2008, www.bloomberg.com/apps/news?pid=20601039&refer =columnist_hassett&sid=a3nzWYaZpoAQ.

42. Hearing Before the Committee on Ways and Means Subcommittee on Oversight, U.S. House of Representatives: "Administration of the First-Time Homebuyer Credit," October 22, 2009, http://www.treas.gov/tigta/congress/ congress_10222009.pdf.

43. Barney Frank, "The Case for a Housing Rescue," *Washington Post*, March 9, 2008, www.washingtonpost.com/ wp-dyn/content/article/2008/03/07/AR200803070 2896.html.

44. Edmund L. Andrews, "My Personal Credit Crisis," *New York Times*, May 14, 2009, www.nytimes.com/2009/ 05/17/magazine/17foreclosure-t.html?%20r=1.

45. Megan McArdle, "The Road to Bankruptcy," *The Atlantic*, May 21, 2009, http://meganmcardle.theatlantic.com/ archives/2009/05/the_road_to_bankruptcy.php.

46. BasePoint New Release, "New BasePoint Study Finds Fraud Linked to Up to 70% of Early Payment Defaults," February 12, 2007, www.basepointanalytics.com/newsfiles/NR%20-%20 BasePoint%20Finds%20EPD%20Linked%20to%20Fraud %2002-12-2007.pdf.

47. Luigi Guiso, Paola Sapienza, and Luigi Zingales, "Moral and Social Constraints to Strategic Default on Mortgages," Working Paper No. 15145, National Bureau of Economic Research, July 2009.

48. "20% of Homeowners 'Underwater,'" by Les Christie, CNNMoney.com, May 6, 2009, http://money.cnn.com/ 2009/05/05/real_estate/underwater_homeowners/index.h tm; Office of the Chief Economist, Freddie Mac, "Cash-Out Refinance Report, 3Q 2009," www.freddiemac.com/ news/finance/docs/cashout_vol_annual.xls; Ronel Elul, Federal Reserve Bank of Philadelphia, Working Paper No. 09–21, "Securitization and Mortgage Default: Reputation vs. Adverse Selection," September 22, 2009, www.fhfa.gov/webfiles/15052/website_elul.pdf.

49. Martin Feldstein, "How to Save an 'Underwater' Mortgage," *Wall Street Journal*, August 7, 2009.

50. Luigi Guiso, Paola Sapienza, and Luigi Zingales. "Moral and Social Constraints to Strategic Default on Mortgages," NBER Working Paper No. 15145, July 2009, www.nber.org/papers/w15145.pdf, Working Paper No. 09–21, "Securitization and Mortgage Default: Reputation vs. Adverse Selection," by Ronel Elul, Federal Reserve Bank of Philadelphia, September 22, 2009, www.fhfa.gov/web-files/15052/website_elul.pdf.

51. "Homeowner Affordability and Stability Plan," U.S. Department of the Treasury, February 18, 2009, www.treas.gov/press/releases/tg33.htm.

52. Tami Luhby, "Half of 'Rescued' Borrowers Still Default," CNNMoney.com, December 8, 2008, http://money.cnn.com/2008/12/08/news/economy/ mortgage_summit/index.htm.

53. Eric Weiner, "Why Not Just Walk Away from a Home?" NPR, February 13, 2008, www.npr.org/templates/story/story.php?storyId=18958049 ; James R. Hagerty and Nick Timiraos, "Debtor's

Dilemma: Pay the Mortgage or Walk Away," *Wall Street Journal*, December 17, 2009, http://online.wsj.com/article/SB126100260600594531.html.

54. Christopher L. Foote, Kristopher Gerardi, and Paul S. Willen, "Negative Equity and Foreclosure: Theory and Evidence," *Public Policy Discussion Papers*, No. 08–3, Federal Reserve Bank of Boston, www.bos.frb.org/economic/ppdp/2008/ppdp0803.pdf.

55. Barack Obama, "The Action Americans Need," *Washington Post*, February 5, 2009, www.washingtonpost.com/wp-dyn/content/article/2009/02/04/AR2009020403174_pf.html.

56. Tom Baldwin and Philip Webster, "Barack Obama: We Must Spend Our Way Out of Recession," *The Times*, January 9, 2009, www.timesonline.co.uk/tol/news/world/us_and_americas/article5478754.ece; Philip Elliott, "New Obama Plans: 'Spend Our Way Out' of Downturn," Breitbart Newswires, December 8, 2009, www.breitbart.com/article.php?id=D9CF8SIO0.

57. "Business Cycle Expansions and Contractions," NBER, http://www.nber.org/cycles.html.

58. Christina Romer and Jared Bernstein, "The Job Impact of the American Recovery and Reinvestment Plan," January 9, 2009, http://otrans.3cdn.net/45593e8ecbd339d074_l3m6bt1te.pdf; Bureau of Labor Statistics, News Release, "The Employment Situation—December 2009," www.bls.gov/news.release/pdf/empsit.pdf.

59. Bureau of Labor Statistics, "Unemployed Persons by Industry and Class of Worker, Not Seasonally Adjusted," www.bls.gov/news.release/empsit.t14.htm.

60. As of February 2010, only $74.4 billion of the funds devoted to programs to create jobs had been spent out, giving a cost per job of $116,190 and the number of jobs that should have been created 1.5 million. Recovery Accountability and Transparency Board, www.recovery.gov/Pages/home.aspx;"PINC-10. Wage and Salary Workers—People 15 Years Old and Over, by Total Wage and Salary Income in 2008, Work Experience in 2008, Race, Hispanic Origin, and Sex," Census Bureau, www.census.gov/hhes/www/cpstables/032009/perinc/new 10_001.htm.

61. This is according to the government's own website: http://www.recovery.gov/Pages/home.aspx; "A 40-Year Wish List," *Wall Street Journal*, January 28, 2009, http://online.wsj.com/article/SB1233104665145 22309.html.

62. Robert J. Barro and Charles J. Redlick, "Stimulus Spending Doesn't Work," *Wall Street Journal*, October 1, 2009, http://online.wsj.com/article/SB100014240527487044715 04574440723298786310.html; Recovery.org: "Track the Money," www.recovery.gov/Pages/home.aspx.

63. This highlights an ironic plus of the stimulus: To be a net plus the stimulus must fund projects that otherwise wouldn't take place. The easiest way to identify those is to find projects that are so useless the private sector would never voluntarily fund them. "Getting to $787 Billion," *Wall Street Journal*, February 17, 2009, http://online.wsj.com/public/resources/documents/STIM-

ULUS_FINAL_0217.html; "Recovery.org" Track the Money, www.rccovery.gov/?q=content/agency-allocations; Stimulus Watch, www.stimuluswatch.org/project/ view/1194.

64. "Transcript: Earl Devaney," We Have to Get in on the Front End and Try to Prevent Waste, Fraud and Abuse Before It Happens," *Wall Street Journal*, March 8, 2009, http://online.wsj.com/article/SB1236204901\6003 3243.html.

65. KeithHennessey.com, "Breaking the No Middle Class Tax Increase Pledge (Again)," http://keithhennessey.com/ 2009/11/20/tax-pledge/.

66. Paul Krugman, "Climate of Change," *New York Times*, February 27, 2009, www.nytimes.com/2009/02/27/opin-ion/27krugman.html; Floyd Norris, "It's Hard to Worry About a Deficit 10 Years Out," *New York Times*, August 27, 2009, www.nytimes.com/2009/08/28/business/ economy/28norris.html; Steven Pearlstein, "Tax Fantasies of the Right and Left," *Washington Post*, April 17, 2009, www.washingtonpost.com/wp-dyn/content/article/2009 /04/16/AR2009041604462.html; E. J. Dionne Jr., "Deficit Dodge Ball," *Washington Post*, March 26, 2009, www.washingtonpost.com/wp-dyn/content/article/ 2009/03/25/AR2009032502801.html; Stuart Taylor, "Obama's Left Turn," *National Journal*, March 7, 2009, www.nationaljournal.com/njmagazine/or_20090307_2566 .php; David Leonhardt, "Like Having Medicare? Then Taxes Must Rise," *New York Times*, February 24, 2009, www.nytimes.com/2009/02/25/business/economy/ 25leonhardt.html; Clive Crook, "What War on the Middle Class?" *The Atlantic*, April 2007, www.theatlantic.com/ doc/200704/social-class.

67. Rachel M. Johnson and Jeffrey Rohaly, "The Distribution of Federal Taxes, 2009–12," The Tax Policy Center, August 2009, www.taxpolicycenter.org/ UploadedPDF/411943_distribution_federal.pdf.

68. Kevin Hassett, "Obamacare Tax Frays Middle-Class Vow," Bloomberg.com, October 12, 2009, www.bloomberg.com/ apps/news?pid=20601039&sid=a2dK9UZuFSxQ.

69. Alan Viard, "Denying the Obvious: The Limits of Taxing the Top 3%," September 8, 2009, http://blog.american .com/?p=4619.

70. Congressional Budget Office, "Recent Activity in the Troubled Asset Relief Program," December 2009, www.cbo.gov/ftpdocs/108xx/doc10871/Chapter1.shtml#1 101369; "How Uncle Sam Will Profit from TARP," by Jia Lynn Yang, CNNMoney.com, January 27, 2010, http://money.cnn.com/2010/01/26/news/economy/ tarp_profit.fortune/.

71. Library of Congress, http://thomas.loc.gov/cgi- bin/query/z?c111:H.R.3068; Committee hearings held on bill 7/9/09, www.govtrack.us/congress/bill.xpd?bill=h111–3068. A recent study shows that whether a financial institution got TARP money in the first place was also determined by its connections to people like Mr. Frank. It found that the likelihood of receiving TARP funds is positively related to such things as contacts with members of congressional finance committees. See Ran Duchin and Denis Sosyura, "TARP Investments: Financials and Politics," University of Michigan Working Paper, June 2009.

72. Joan Hoff Wilson, *Herbert Hoover: Forgotten Progressive* (Long Grove, Illinois: Waveland Press, 1992).

73. Amity Shlaes, *The Forgotten Man: A New History of the Great Depression* (New York: HarperCollins, 2007); Christina Romer, "What Ended the Great Depression?" NBER Working Paper No. W3829, September 1991, http://papers.ssrn.com/sol3/papers.cfm?abstract_id= 226730.

74. Leverett S. Lyon, *The National Recovery Administration: an Analysis and Appraisal* (Washington, DC: The Brookings Institution, 1935), 873.

75. "National Affairs: Relief," *Time*, February 25, 1935.

76. Raymond Moley, "Henry George and the Forgotten Man," reprinted from the *Henry George News*, June 1952, www.cooperativeindividualism.org/moley_henry_george _and_forgotten_man.html.

77. George Bush Acceptance Speech, Republican National Convention, August 18, 1988, www.4president.org/speeches/georgebush1988convention. htm.

78. Michael Shermer, "Wronger Than Wrong: Not All Wrong Theories Are Equal," *Scientific American*, November 2006, www.scientificamerican.com/article.cfm?id=wronger -than-wrong.

Chapter Three

1. Michael Kinsley, "Obama, the Wealth Spreader," *TIME*, October 31, 2008, www.time.com/time/magazine/article/0,9171,1855360,00.

html#ixzz0Xh3E0vBi; "Questions Over Obama's Off-the-Cuff Remark," FOX News, October 15, 2008, http://www.foxnews.com/story/0,2933,438302,00.html.

2. U.S. Census Bureau, "Selected Measures of Household Income Dispersion: 1967 to 2008," www.census.gov/hhes/www/income/histinc/IE-1.pdf.

3. Bruno S. Frey and Alois Stutzer, "What Can Economists Learn from Happiness Research?" *Journal of Economic Literature*, American Economic Association, 40, no. 2 (Sept. 2004): 402–435.

4. S. Solnick and D. Hemenway, "Is More Always Better? A Survey on Positional Concerns," *Journal of Economic Behavior and Organization* 37 (1998): 373–383.

5. The Maxwell Poll (2005). Civic Engagement and Inequality, October 2005 (fielded by Syracuse University researchers), merged data set available at www1.maxwell.syr.edu/campbell/programs/Merged_Data_Set/.

6. Richard Layard, *Happiness: Lessons from a New Science* (New York: Penguin Press, 2005), 228.

7. 1996 General Social Survey (GSS).

8. Ibid. This analysis uses a probit estimation to model the likelihood of saying one is "very happy" on a dummy variable, indicating one feels "very successful" or "completely successful," about income and the other demographics listed. The coefficients are evaluated at the margin using the mean value of the regressors.

9. John Mirowsky and Catherine E. Ross, "Aging, Status, and Sense of Control (ASOC), 1995, 1998, 2001," Computer file ICPSR03334-v2 (Columbus: Ohio State University

[producer], 2001/Ann Arbor, MI: Inter-University Consortium for Political and Social Research [distributor], 2005-12-15).

10. J. A. Schumpeter (trans. R. Opie). *The Theory of Economic Development* (Cambridge, MA: Harvard University Press, 1934).

11. Further insight on the subject is provided by the 2009 *Legatum Prosperity Index* (www.prosperity.com/), which seeks a more holistic measure of prosperity that captures both objective and subjective levels of wealth and well-being.

12. James A. Davis, Tom W. Smith, and Peter V. Marsden, *General Social Surveys, 1972–2004* (Storrs, CT: The Roper Center for Public Opinion Research, University of Connecticut, 2004).

13. Known as the "Easterlin paradox," this finding stood for several years. Richard A. Easterlin, "Does Economic Growth Improve the Human Lot?" in Paul A. David and Melvin W. Reder, eds., *Nations and Households in Economic Growth: Essays in Honor of Moses Abramovitz* (New York: Academic Press, 1974). Lately, however, economists Betsey Stevenson and Justin Wolfers questioned it, citing Gallup public opinion surveys from around the world. They conclude that rising national income levels do indeed raise national levels of subjective well-being (David Leonhardt, "Maybe Money Does Buy Happiness After All," *New York Times*, April 16, 2008, www.nytimes.com/2008/04/16/business/16leonhardt.html ?_r=1).

14. Philip Brickman, Dan Coates, and Ronnie Janoff-Bulman, "Lottery Winners and Accident Victims: Is Happiness

Relative?" *Journal of Personality and Social Psychology* 36, no. 8 (1978): 917–927, http://education.ucsb.edu/janeconoley/ed197/documents/brickman_lotterywinnersandaccidentvictims.pdf.

15. Panel Study of Income Dynamics (PSID), Wave XXXII Computer File (Ann Arbor, MI: ICPSR, 2001), http://simba.isr.umich.edu; Arthur Brooks, *Gross National Happiness* (New York: Basic Books, 2008), 167–168.

16. Bernard M. S. Van Praag and Paul Frijters, "The Measurement of Welfare and Well-Being," in eds. Daniel Kahneman, Ed Diener, and Norbert Schwartz, *Well-Being: The Foundation of Hedonic Psychology* (New York: Russell Sage, 1999), 413–433.

17. 2004 GSS.

18. The Maxwell Poll, www1.maxwell.syr.edu/campbell/programs/The_Maxwell_Poll/.

19. This comparison uses unweighted data. When the data are weighted, the gap is 46 percent to 28 percent.

20. Robert Moffitt, "The Effect of Taxation on Labor Supply in Industrialized Countries: A Conference," www.irp.wisc.edu/publications/focus/pdfs/foc114b.pdf; Thomas Lemieux, Bernard Fortin, and Pierre Fréchette, "The Effect of Taxes on Labor Supply in the Underground Economy," *The American Economic Review* 84, no. 1 (1994): 231–254.

21. Kevin Hassett, "Dollar's Demise Traces Roots to U.S. Tax Trap," Bloomberg.com, November 16, 2009, www.bloomberg.com/apps/news?pid=20601039&sid=aWwPrRxeEoyk.

22. Source: Tax Foundation,
www.taxfoundation.org/blog/show/24981.html.

23. See Kevin Hassett and Alex Brill (2007). "Revenue-
Maximizing Corporate Income Taxes," AEI Working Paper
No. 137. Coefficients are taken from Table 5, p. 16. The
39 percent rate reflects the sum of the top federal corporate tax rate and the average state corporate tax rate,
adjusting for the fact that state corporate taxes are
deductible at the federal level. The downward adjustment
to 26 percent would raise GDP by 0.8 percent. Arthur B.
Laffer, "The Laffer Curve: Past, Present, and Future,"
Heritage Foundation, June 1, 2004,
www.heritage.org/Research/Taxes/bg1765.cfm.

24. John Sabelhaus, "Equity and Bond Ownership in America, 2008," Investment Company Institute and the
Securities Industry and Financial Markets Association,
www.ici.org/pdf/rpt_08_equity_owners.pdf.

25. The 2000 Social Capital Community Benchmark Survey;
2004 GSS; R. E. Lucas, A. E. Clark, Y. Georgellis, and E.
Diener, "Reexamining Adaptation and the Setpoint Model
of Happiness: Reactions to Changes in Marital Status,"
Journal of Personality and Social Psychology 84 (2003):
527–539.

26. 1983 GSS.

27. Victor Frankl, *Man's Search for Meaning* (New York:
Pocket Books, 1984).

28. International Social Survey Programme 2002. "Family
and Changing Gender Roles III (ISSP 2002)" Gesis Data
Archive, www.gesis.org/en/services/data/survey-data/
issp/modules-study-overview/family-changing-gender

-roles/2002/. The only European country that edges the
United States is Austria. (Percentages of population
describing themselves as "completely satisfied": Germany
East: 7.7; Germany West: 10.2; UK: 10.9; U.S.: 15.5; Austria: 17.7; France: 10.6; Spain: 5.3).

29. Arthur C. Brooks, *Gross National Happiness*, 157–158;
Arthur Brooks, "I Love My Work," *The American*
(Sept./Oct. 2007), www.american.com/archive/2007/
september-october-magazine-contents/i-love-my
-work/?searchterm=arthur brooks.

30. Arthur C. Brooks, *Social Entrepreneurship: A Modern
Approach to Social Value Creation* (Upper Saddle River,
NJ: Prentice-Hall, 2008); 2002 GSS.

31. James Joyner, "European Youth Unemployment Creating
Lost Generation?" *New Atlantacist*, July 14, 2009,
www.acus.org/new_atlanticist/european-youth-unemploy
ment-creating-lost-generation.

32. Brett W. Pelham, "Business Owners Richer in Well-Being
Than Other Job Types," September 16, 2009,
www.gallup.com/poll/122960/Business-Owners-
Richer-Job-Types.aspx?CSTS=alert; George J. Borjas, "Job
Satisfaction, Wages, and Unions," *The Journal of Human
Resources*, 14, no. 1 (1979), www.jstor.org/stable/145536.

33. Ute Stephan and Ulrike Roesler, "Health of
Entrepreneurs Versus Employees in a National Represen-
tative Sample," *Journal of Occupational and
Organizational Psychology* (September 2010): 717–738.

34. Jutta J. Allmendinger, J. Richard Hackman, and Erin V.
Lehman, "Life and Work in Symphony Orchestras: An
Interim Report of Research Findings," Report No. 7.

Cross National Study of Symphony Orchestras
(Cambridge, MA: Harvard University, 1994).

35. Brian M. Carney and Isaac Getz, *Freedom, Inc.: Free Your Employees and Let Them Lead Your Business to Higher Productivity, Profits, and Growth* (New York: Crown Business, 2009).

36. Ellen J. Langer and Judith Rodin, "The Effects of Choice and Enhanced Personal Responsibility for the Aged: A Field Experiment in an Institutional Setting." *Journal of Personality and Social Psychology* 34 (1976): 191–198.

37. Heritage Foundation, *2010 Index of Economic Freedom,* www.heritage.org/Index/.

38. See Arthur Brooks, *Gross National Happiness,* p. 222 for a reference to the *Wall Street Journal* and Heritage Foundation's Index of Economic Freedom (2007).

39. "Time Series Chart of US Government Spending," www.usgovernmentspending.com/charts.html. (Note that spending levels include state and local spending.)

40. The Pew Research Center's polls in the final months of 2009 show that opposition to proposed health care reform has outweighed support. In September, 42 percent favored the health care plans being discussed in Congress; in November, 38 percent did. (From Karlyn Bowman, "More Health Care, But Less Government," Forbes.com, December 14, 2009); a Rasmussen poll in December 21, 2009, showed 41 percent of Americans favored the health reform legislation in the Senate and 55 percent opposed it (www.rasmussenreports.com/public_content/politics/current_events/healthcare/september_2009/health_care_reform); Jeremy Twitchell, "Harry Reid: Reform a 'Moral

Issue' with Financial Benefits," *Las Vegas Sun,* September 1, 2009, www.lasvegassun.com/news/2009/sep/01/ harry-reid-reform-moral-issue-financial-benefits/; Douglas Holtz-Eaking, "All's Not Fair in Health Reform Bills," *Boston Globe,* December 10, 2009, www.boston .com/bostonglobe/editorial_opinion/oped/articles/2009/ 12/10/alls_not_fair_in_health_reform_bills/.

41. Joe Antos, "Troublesome Direction of Health Reform," NationalJournal.com, November 16, 2009, www.aei.org/ article/101319.

42. Arthur Brooks, "Why Government Health Care Keeps Falling in the Polls," *Wall Street Journal,* October 26, 2009.

43. Carmen DeNavas-Walt, Bernadette D. Proctor, and Jessica C. Smith, "Income, Poverty, and Health Insurance Coverage in the United States: 2008," U.S. Census Bureau, September 2009, www.census.gov/prod/2009pubs/ p60–236.pdf.

44. Martin Feldstein, "Obamacare's Nasty Surprise," *Washington Post,* November 6, 2009, www.washingtonpost.com/ wp-dyn/content/article/2009/11/05/AR200911 0504327.html.

Chapter Four

1. Rasmussen Reports, "51% View Tea Parties Favorably, Political Class Strongly Disagrees," April 20, 2009, www.rasmussenreports.com/public_content/politics/ general_politics/april_2009/51_view_tea_parties_ favorably_political_class_strongly_disagrees; AEI Political

Report, Volume 6, Issue 2, February 2010,
http://www.aei.org/docLib/Political-Report-Feb-2010.pdf.

2. See www.thcneweditor.com/index.php?/archives/
9472-CNN-Reporter-Get-Taken-To-Task-by-Chicago
-Tea-Party-Crowd.html.

3. FOX News/Opinion Dynamics Poll, January 2010: "Based
on what you know about the health care reform legislation being considered right now, do you favor or oppose
the plan?"; Kaiser/Harvard/NPR, The Role of Health
Care Interest Groups Survey, August 2009: "Do you think
that these protests (against the health care plan at town
hall meetings with members of Congress) are doing more
harm than good or more good than harm?"; Kaiser/
Harvard/NPR The Role of Health Care Interest Groups
Survey, August 2009: "Do you think the protests (against
the health care plan) at the town hall meetings (with
members of Congress) were mainly the result of individual citizens coming together to express their views, or do
you think they were mainly the result of coordination by
health care interest groups?"

4. RealClearPolitics.com, "Massachusetts Senate–Special
Election,"
www.realclearpolitics.com/epolls/2010/senate/ma/
massachusetts_senate_special_election-1144.html.

5. Kevin A. Hassett, "Centerfold Senator Is Stud on
Economics as Well," January 25, 2010, Bloomberg.com,
www.bloomberg.com/apps/news?pid=20601039sid=avjLU
kG20aFA.

6. CNNPolitics.com, "CNN Poll: 3 of 4 Americans Say Much
of Stimulus Money Wasted," January 25, 2010,
www.cnn.com/2010/POLITICS/01/25/poll.stimulus

.money/index.html?hpt=T2; AEI Political Report, Volume 6, Issue 2, February 2010, www.aei.org/docLib/Political -Report-Feb-2010.pdf.

7. James Madison, *Federalist*, No. 10, 1788.

8. Ayers, McHenry & Associates, 2009.

9. Abraham Lincoln speech at New Haven, Connecticut, March 6, 1860, http://history.hanover.edu/courses/excerpts/165lincolnne whaven.html.

10. "For Obama, Taxes Are About Fairness," *Wall Street Journal*, August 19, 2008, http://online.wsj.com/article/SB12191011776795 1201.html?mod=todays_columnists.

11. IRS, "Returns with Positive Adjusted Gross Income" table, www.irs.gov/pub/irs-soi/07in01etr.xls.

12. "Tax Units With Zero or Negative Tax Liability, 2009– 2019," Table T09–0333, Tax Policy Center, www.taxpolicycenter.org/numbers/displayatab.cfm?Docid =2408&DocTypeID=7.

13. IRS, "Returns with Positive Adjusted Gross Income" table, www.irs.gov/pub/irs-soi/07in01etr.xls and author's calculations; "How Do Americans Feel About Taxes Today? Tax Foundation's 2009 Survey of U.S. Attitudes on Taxes, Government Spending and Wealth Distribution," April 2009, No. 166, www.taxfoundation.org/files/sr166.pdf.

14. In the Gospels, Jesus says, "Again I tell you, it is easier for a camel to go through the eye of a needle than for a rich man to enter the kingdom of God" (Matthew 19:24);

"Blessed are you poor, for yours is the kingdom of God" (Luke 6:20); and "The poor man died and was carried by the angels to Abraham's bosom. The rich man also died and was buried; and in Hades, being in torment, he lifted up his eyes, and saw Abraham far off and Lazarus in his bosom" (Luke 16:22–23).

15. See Professor Walzer's outstanding essay on this subject, "Does the Free Market Corrode Moral Character?" at www.templeton.org/market/.

16. Gerard Alexander, "Why Are Liberals So Condescending?" *Washington Post*, February 7, 2010, www.washingtonpost.com/wp-dyn/content/article/2010/02/04/AR2010020403698.html.

17. A September 2009 study in *Perspectives on Politics* by Leslie McCall and Lane Kenworthy, titled "Americans' Social Policy Preferences in the Era of Rising Inequality," finds that Americans are not insensitive to the trend of rising levels of income inequality in this country. But they do not believe that income redistribution by government is the solution. Instead, they favor expanding education in response to their increasing concerns about inequality.

18. See Paul Sinclair, "Grameen Micro-Credit & How to End Poverty from the Roots Up," 2006, http://oneworldonepeople.org/articles/World%20Poverty/Grameen.htm.

19. Muhammad Yunus, *Banker to the Poor: Micro-Lending and the Battle Against World Poverty* (New York: PublicAffairs, 2003); David Bornstein, *The Price of a Dream: The Story of the Grameen Bank* (New York: Oxford University Press, 2005).

20. Dambisa Moyo, *Why Aid Is Not Working and How There Is a Better Way for Africa* (New York: Farrar, Straus and Giroux, 2009).

21. As Michael Novak has been arguing since the 1980s, "The revolution is moral or not at all." Michael Novak, "Introduction: The Revolution Is Moral or Not at All," in eds. Peter L. Berger and Michael Novak, *Speaking to the Third World: Essays on Democracy and Development* (Washington, DC: American Enterprise Institute, 1985).

22. U.S. Census Bureau, "Poverty: 2008 Highlights," www.census.gov/hhes/www/poverty/poverty08/pov08hi.ht ml; The 2010 Hunger Report defines asset poverty thus:

> A measure of economic security and mobility based on household net worth. Where *net worth* is defined as the total value of all assets, such as a house or a business, minus any liabilities, such as debts. A household is asset poor if it has insufficient net worth to subsist at the federal poverty level for three months in the absence of income. Thus, an asset poor household would not have enough savings or wealth to provide for basic needs during extended periods of economic hardship, such as a sudden job loss or a medical emergency.

> www.hungerreport.org/2010/data/income-security/ 146-asset-poverty, www.hungerreport.org/2010/data/income-security/ 115-children-and-poverty.

23. Address Before a Joint Session of Congress on the State of the Union, January 25, 1988, www.reagan.utexas.edu/archives/speeches/1988/012588d. htm; U.S. Department of Health and Human Services: Administration for Children and Families, Caseload Data

1960–1999, www.acf.hhs.gov/programs/ofa/data-reports/caseload/caseload_archive.html; in 1970, 3 percent of the population was on welfare. In 1996, this had risen to 3.2 percent. See Population Estimates Program, Population Division, U.S. Census Bureau, www.census.gov/popest/archives/1990s/popclockest.txt.

24. The legislation to reform welfare was the Personal Responsibility and Work Opportunity Reconciliation Act of 1996 (PRWORA). The government no longer required recipients to be unmarried and unemployed. On the contrary, people had to work to receive benefits, if at all possible. The reforms also substituted a system in which 80 percent of support had been dispersed in checks to recipients with one in which about 60 percent of funds went directly to providing needed services. The most prominent changes, however, were the time limits placed on recipients. All states adopted a five-year lifetime limit on welfare support, and many states also imposed shorter limits on periods of continuous support. The main welfare program's name changed to reflect these limits, from Aid to Families with Dependent Children (AFDC) to Temporary Aid to Needy Families (TANF). See Children's Defense Fund, "Edelman Decries President's Betrayal of Promise 'Not to Hurt Children,'" July 31, 1996; Center on Budget and Policy Priorities, "Urban Institute Study Confirms that Welfare Bills Would Increase Child Poverty," 1996, www.cbpp.org/URBAN726.HTM; U.S. Bureau of the Census, Poverty in the United States: 1999; Income, Poverty, and Health Insurance Coverage: 2003, www.census.gov/prod/2004pubs/p60–226.pdf. John J. DiIulio Jr., "Older & Wiser?" *The Weekly Standard*, 011, no. 1 (2005).

25. See Charles Murray, *Losing Ground: American Social Policy, 1950–1980* (New York: Basic Books, 1995).

26. For a concise summary of this research, see Nick Schulz and Arnold Kling, *From Poverty to Prosperity Intangible Assets, Hidden Liabilities and the Lasting Triumph over Scarcity* (New York: Encounter Books, 2009).

27. Democracy Corps Poll, August 2006.

28. Philip Levy, "Trade: The Unsung Hero," *The American,* October 6, 2009, www.american.com/archive/2009/october/trade-the-unsung-hero; Philip Levy, "Does Trade Policy Matter?" *AEI Outlook Series,* October 2008, http://www.aei.org/outlook/28708.

29. World Bank, Country Brief: China, http://web.worldbank.org/WBSITE/EXTERNAL/ COUNTRIES/EASTASIAPACIFICEXT/CHINAEXTN/0,, menuPK:318960~pagePK:141132~piPK:141107~theSite PK:318950,00.html; Arthur C. Brooks, "Don't Live Simply," *AEI Articles* and *Commentary,* September 15, 2008, www.aei.org/article/28626.

30. Philip I. Levy, "Economic Integration and Incipient Democracy," AEI Papers & Studies, March 26, 2008, www.aei.org/paper/27707.

31. The NAFTA violation came as a consequence of the 2009 termination of a cross-border, long-distance trucking demonstration project. The administration has said it plans to develop a new trucking project in 2010. See The White House, Office of the Press Secretary, March 16, 2009, Press Briefing by Press Secretary Robert Gibbs, www.whitehouse.gov/the_press_office/Briefing-by-WH-Press-Secretary-Gibbs-3-16-09; Peter Whoriskey and

Anne Kornblut, "U.S. to Impose Tariff on Tires from China," *Washington Post*, September 12, 2009, www.washingtonpost.com/wp-dyn/content/article/2009/09/11/AR2009091103957.html; Neena Shenai, "The Importance of Free Trade," Forbes.com, June 9, 2009, www.forbes.com/2009/06/08/free-trade-obama-opinions-contributors-protectionism.html.

32. Sitaram Yechury, "No Blood for Oil, Mr. President!" *Akhbár*, October 2001, www.indowindow.com/akhbar/article.php?article=53&category=10&issue=12.

33. *International Herald Tribune*, September 25, 1997; *Sunday Times*, March 24, 1996; Ben Arnoldy, "In Afghanistan, Taliban kills more civilians than US," *Christian Science Monitor*, July 31, 2009.

34. World Economic Forum, The Global Competitiveness Report, 2009–2010, www.weforum.org/pdf/GCR09/GCR20092010full report.pdf.

35. Gallup, www.gallup.com/poll/145238/Congress-Job -Approval-Rating-Worst-Gallup-History.aspx. Gallup, http://www.gallup.com/poll/28795/Low-Trust-Federal -Government-Rivals-Watergate-Era-Levels.aspx; http://www.gallup.com/poll/122897/Americans-Trust -Legislative-Branch-Record-Low.aspx.

36. Gallup polls: www.gallup.com/poll/122897/Americans -Trust-Legislative-Branch-Record-Low.aspx; www.gallup.com/poll/110458/Trust-Government -Remains-Low.aspx; National Data Program for the Social Sciences polls, http://publicdata.norc.org/webview/velocity?study=http%3A%2F%2Fpublicdata.norc.org%3A 80%2Fobj%2FfStudy%2F4697&v=2&mode=documen

tation&submode=variable&variable=http%3A%2F%2Fpu
blicdata.norc.org%3A80%2Fobj%2FfVariable%2F4697_V
421; http://publicdata.norc.org/webview/
velocity?study=http%3A%2F%2Fpublicdata.norc.org%3A
80%2Fobj%2FfStudy%2F4697&v=2&mode=documen
tation&submode=variable&variable=http%3A%2F%2Fpu
blicdata.norc.org%3A80%2Fobj%2FfVariable%2F4697_
V426; http://publicdata.norc.org/webview/
velocity?study=http%3A%2F%2Fpublicdata.norc.org%3A
80%2Fobj%2FfStudy%2F4697&v=2&mode=documen
tation&submode=variable&variable=http%3A%2F%2Fpu
blicdata.norc.org%3A80%2Fobj%2FfVariable%2F4697
_V428; http://publicdata.norc.org/webview/velocity
?study=http%3A%2F%2Fpublicdata.norc.org%3A80%2
Fobj%2FfStudy%2F4697&v=2&mode=documentation
&submode=variable&variable=http%3A%2F%2Fpublic-
data.norc.org%3A80%2Fobj%2FfVariable%2F4697_V429.
See also Gallup polls, www.gallup.com/poll/122897/
Americans-Trust-Legislative-Branch-Record-Low.aspx.

37. PollingReport.com, www.pollingreport.com/cong_rep.htm.

38. Ronald Reagan, "The Republican Party & the Conservative Movement—On Losing," *National Review's*
"Flashback from the Archives," www.nationalreview.com/
flashback/reagan200406061525.asp.

39. David Frum, Henry Olsen, and Sam Tanenhaus, "Republican Recovery," AEI *On the Issues*, November 25, 2008,
www.aei.org/issue/28991.

Index